P9-CLU-550

PRE-WRITING PRACTICE

This section contains a variety of exercises that will help your child develop the eye-hand coordination and fine motor skills that are necessary to learn to write clearly. The exercises are arranged in order of increasing difficulty, so encourage your child to work from the beginning to the end of this section. The exercises start off with the goal of guiding a pencil or crayon along a path to reach a destination. The exercises then focus on tracing shapes. The final pages of this section use a more formal approach to practice the skills needed for manuscript writing. All of these activities are designed to get your child ready to write. He or she will need these skills for the next section of this workbook, which includes a focus on tracing and writing the letters of the alphabet.

Trace the lines from **left** to **right**.

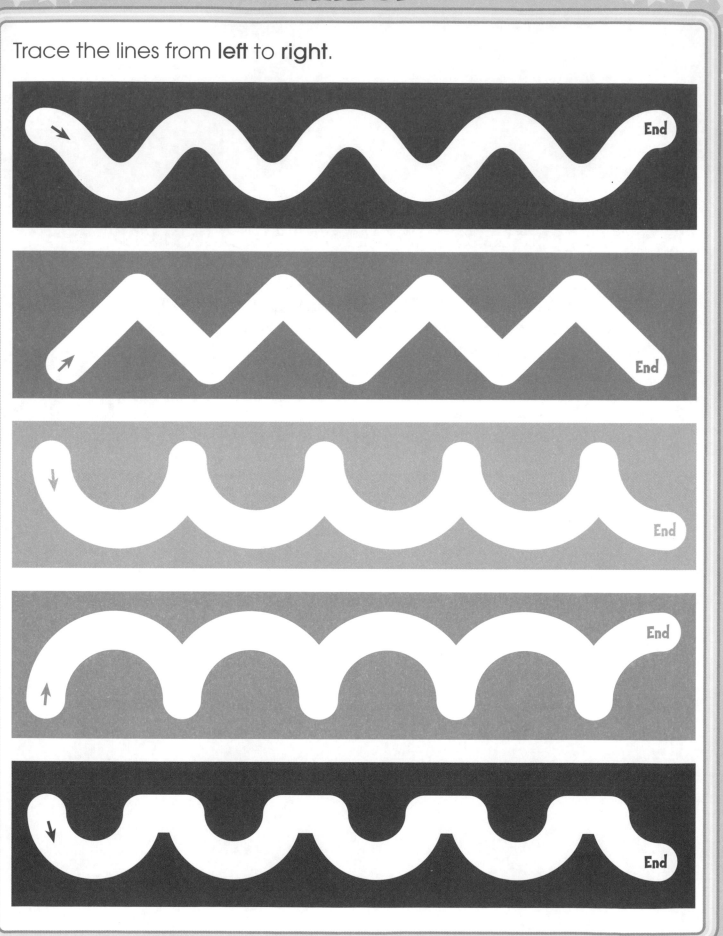

Help the hippos get below.
Trace the path.

End

3

Help the train get to the station on time.
Trace the path.

End

Get to the center of the shell.
Trace the path.

Tracing

Look at how much this caterpillar has eaten.
Trace the path.

End

Help the farmer pick the corn.
Trace the path.

End

Follow the lightning bolt.
Trace the path.

8

Help get the gold out of the mine.
Trace the path.

9

Get to the center of the web.
Trace the path.

End

10

Help the ant get through the tunnel.
Trace the path.

11

Help the bee get to each flower.
Trace the path.

End

Help the plane land.
Trace the path.

End

Help the frog leap across the lily pads.
Trace the path.

End

14

Help find the missing puppy.
Trace the path.

End

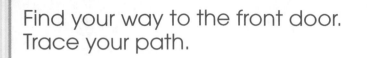

Find your way to the front door.
Trace your path.

End

Help the rocket get to the planet.
Trace the path.

Tracing

Follow the roller coaster around the twists and turns.
Trace the path.

RIDE THE
LOOP-THE-LOOP

End

Get to the center of the lollipop.
Trace the path.

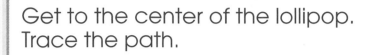

End

This diver found the sunken treasure.
Trace the path.

End

20

Learn the **shapes** by tracing the dotted lines.

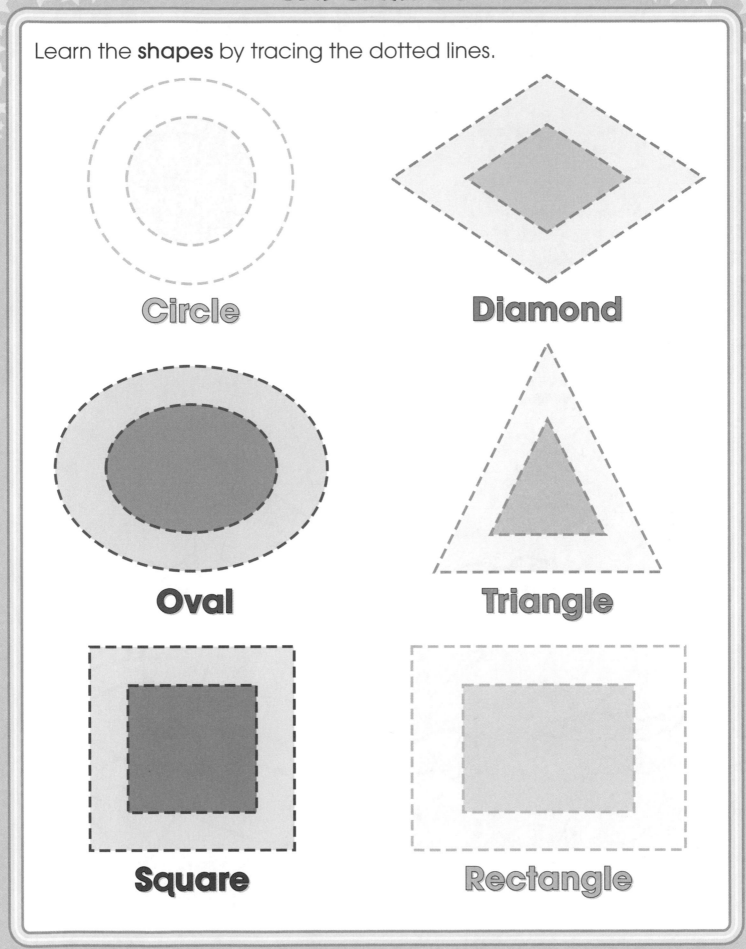

Circle

Diamond

Oval

Triangle

Square

Rectangle

Practice tracing **circles**. Then color the picture.

Practice tracing **diamonds**. Then color the picture.

Tracing

Practice tracing **ovals**. Then color the picture.

Practice tracing **triangles**. Then color the picture.

SQUARES

Practice tracing **squares**. Then color the picture.

Practice tracing **rectangles**. Then color the picture.

Practice tracing lines from **top** to **bottom**.

28

Practice tracing slanted lines from **left** to **right**.

Practice tracing slanted lines from **right** to **left**.

Practice tracing **curved** lines.

Practice tracing **circles**.

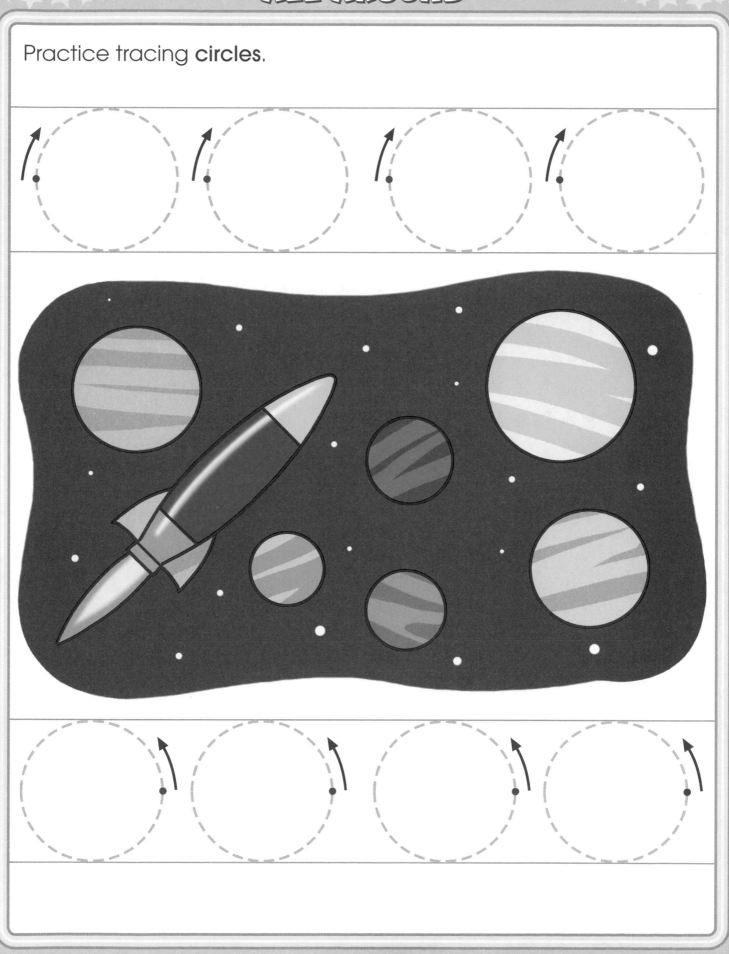

ALPHABET

This section will teach your child to recognize the letters of the alphabet, which is an essential first step in learning to read. Here are some tips to help your child get the most from this section:

• To help your child learn the letters in alphabetical order, encourage your child to work from the beginning to the end of this section.

• Explain to your child that there is an uppercase and lowercase version of each letter.

• Have your child say each letter out loud.

• The ready-to-color picture representing each letter will provide coloring fun. Encourage your child to pronounce each word as they color the picture, which will help reinforce beginning sounds, another important reading readiness skill.

• The manuscript writing component will give your child an opportunity to practice tracing and writing the letters of the alphabet. The pages include the proper starting points for each letter stroke. Encourage your child to follow the arrows, which will help your child develop legible handwriting.

THE ALPHABET

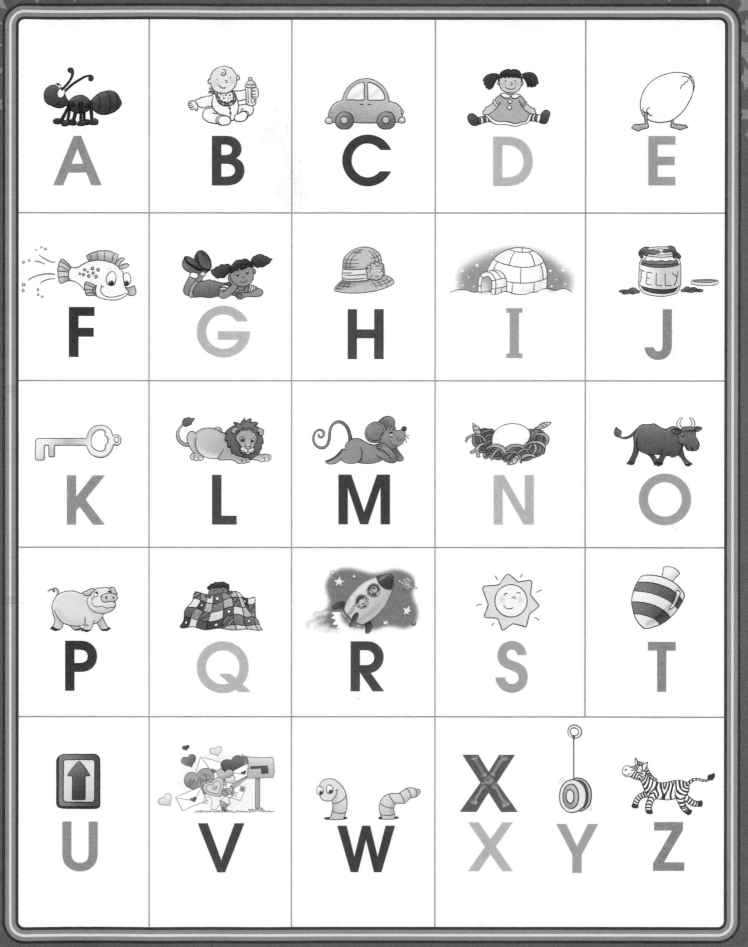

A B C D E

F G H I J

K L M N O

P Q R S T

U V W X Y Z

Alphabet

A
ALLIGATOR

Color the picture.
Trace **A**. Then write **A**.

a
anteater

Color the picture.
Trace **a**. Then write **a**.

B

BIRDS

Color the picture.
Trace **B**. Then write **B**.

b

butterfly

Color the picture.
Trace **b**. Then write **b**.

Alphabet

C

CAT

Color the picture.
Trace **C**. Then write **C**.

C

clown

Color the picture.
Trace c. Then write c.

D

DOG

Color the picture.
Trace **D**. Then write **D**.

d
drummer

Color the picture.
Trace **d**. Then write **d**.

E

EIGHT

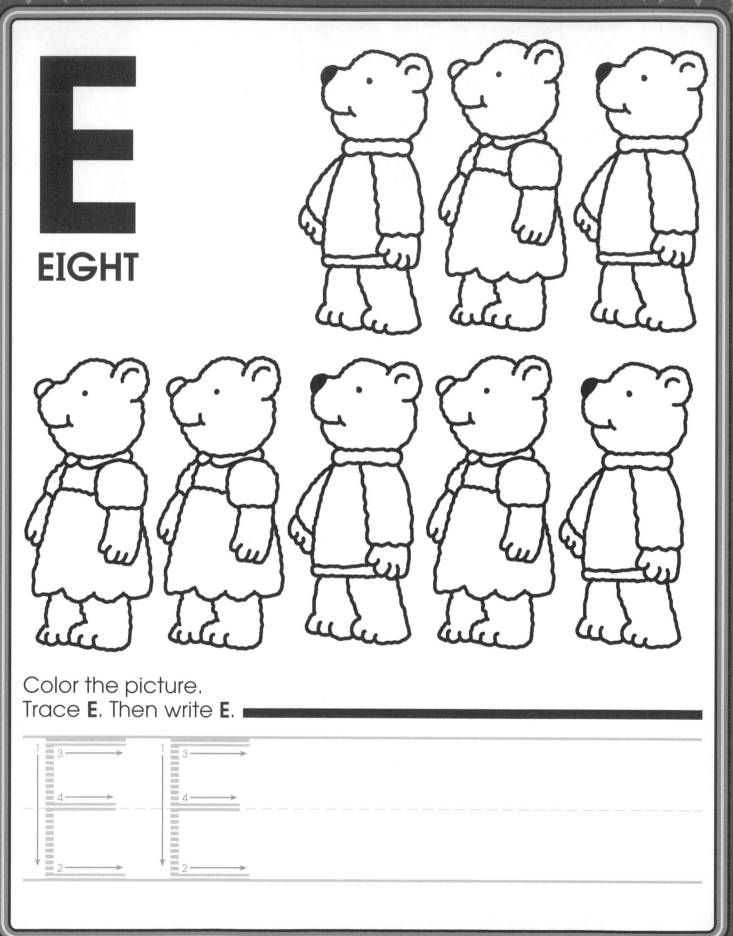

Color the picture.
Trace **E**. Then write **E**.

e

elephant

Color the picture.
Trace **e**. Then write **e**.

Alphabet

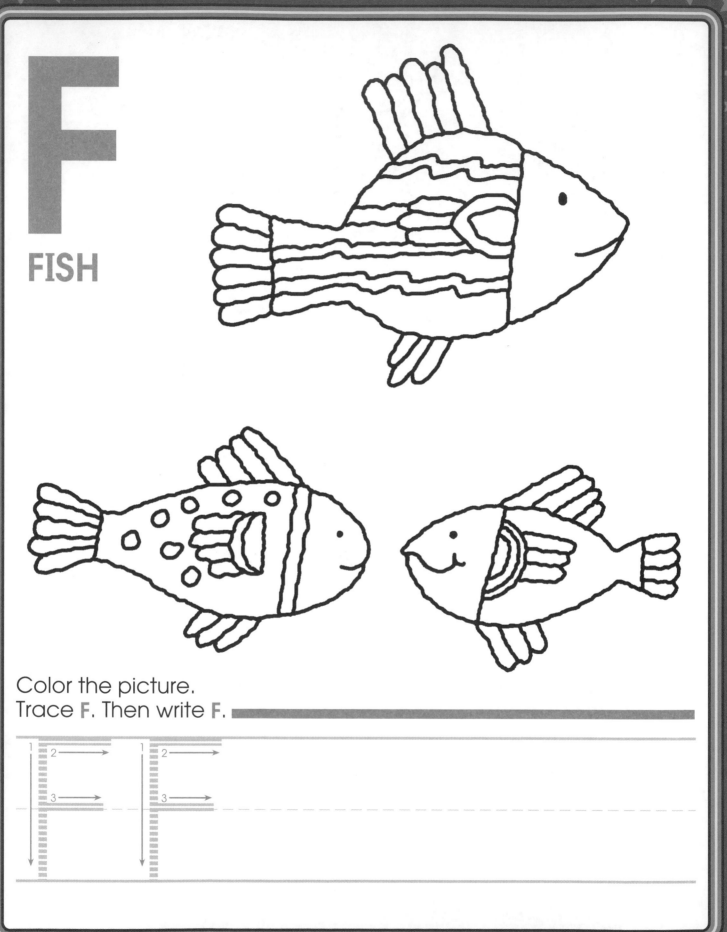

F

FISH

Color the picture.
Trace **F**. Then write **F**.

f

flowers

Color the picture.
Trace **f**. Then write **f**.

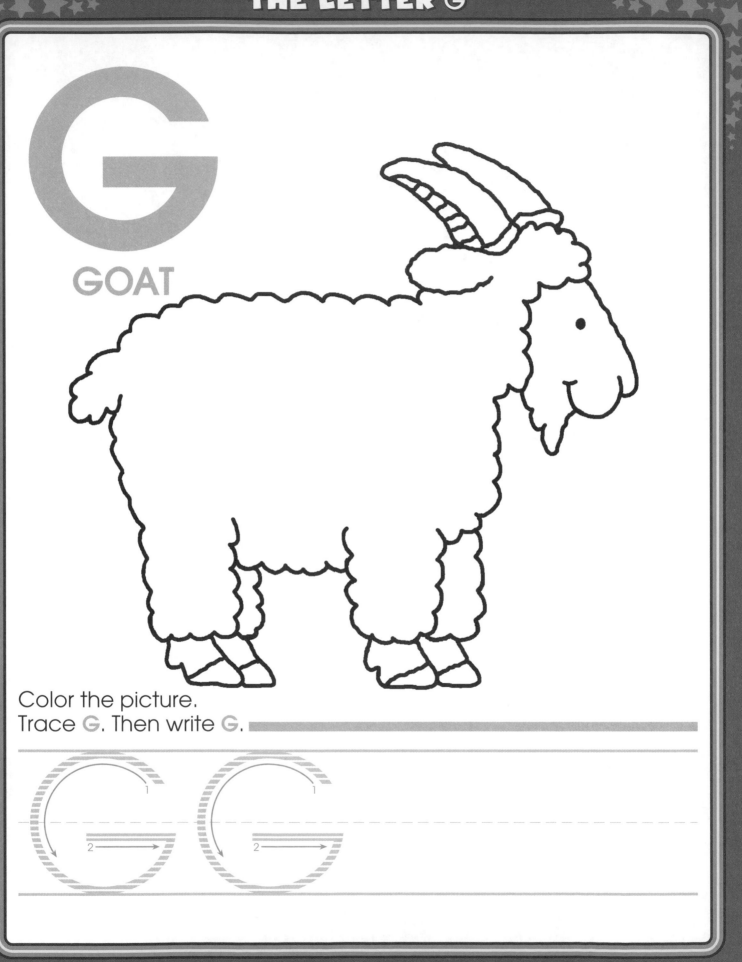

G

GOAT

Color the picture.
Trace G. Then write G.

grandmother

Color the picture.
Trace **g**. Then write **g**.

H

HEN

Color the picture.
Trace **H**. Then write **H**.

h

horse

Color the picture.
Trace **h**. Then write **h**.

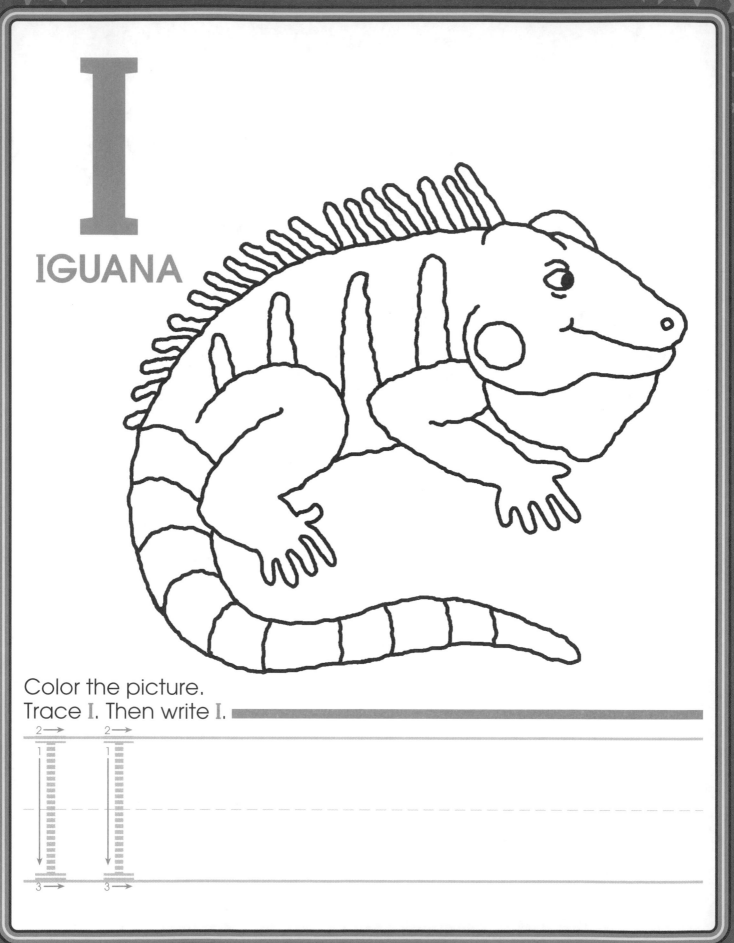

I

IGUANA

Color the picture.
Trace I. Then write I.

i

ink

Color the picture.
Trace i. Then write i.

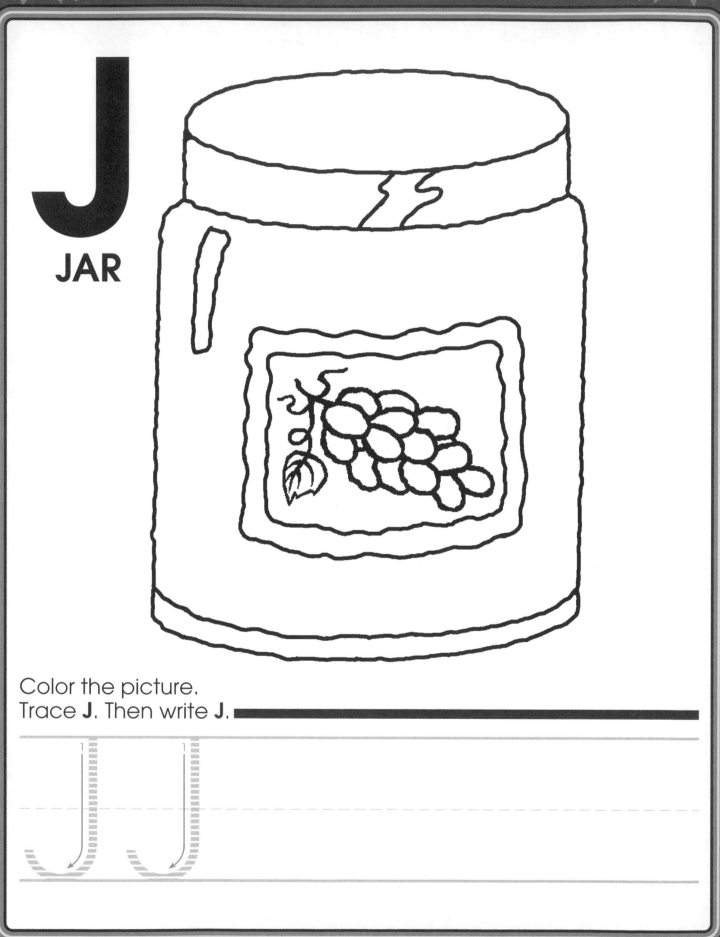

J
JAR

Color the picture.
Trace **J**. Then write **J**.

j

jet

Color the picture.
Trace **j**. Then write **j**.

K
KANGAROO

Color the picture.
Trace K. Then write K.

k

kite

Color the picture.
Trace k. Then write k.

LEAVES

Color the picture.
Trace L. Then write L.

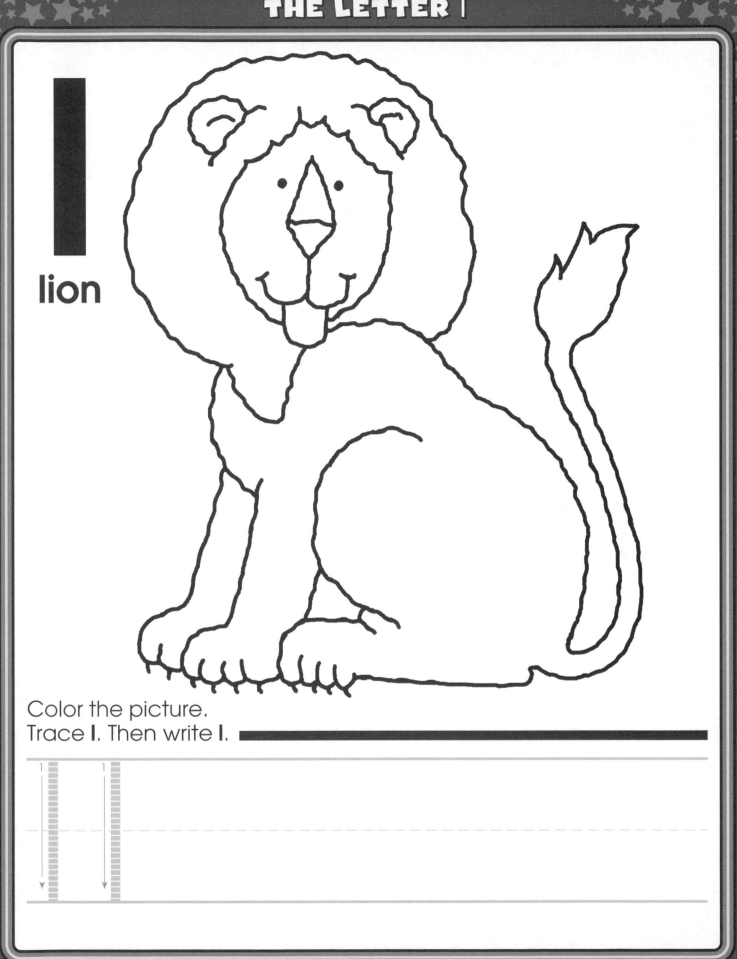

lion

Color the picture.
Trace l. Then write l.

M
MONKEY

Color the picture.
Trace **M**. Then write **M**.

m

moon

Color the picture.
Trace **m**. Then write **m**.

N
NEST

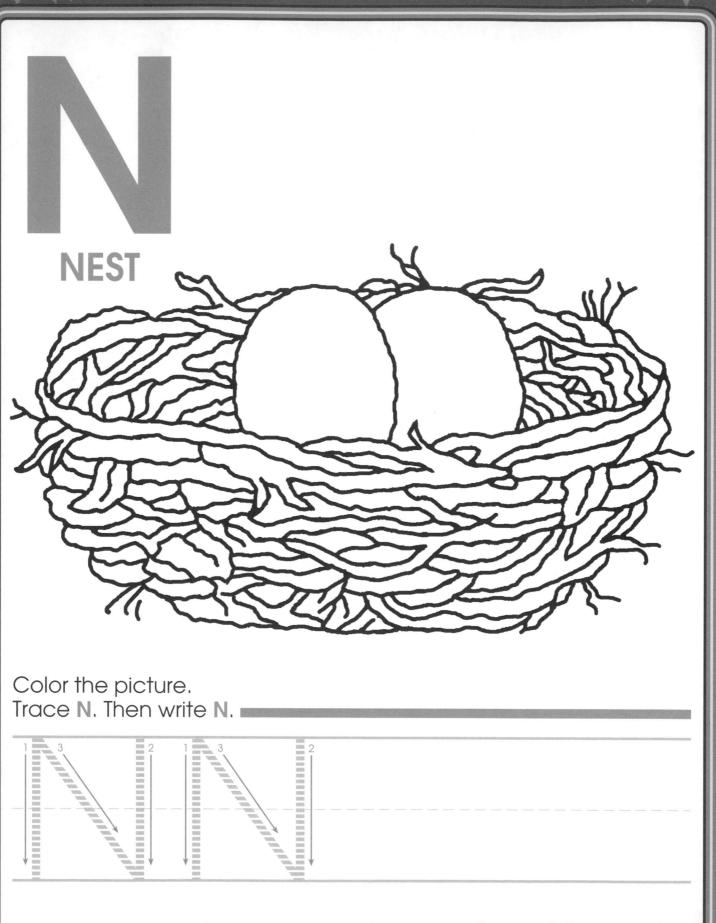

Color the picture.
Trace **N**. Then write **N**.

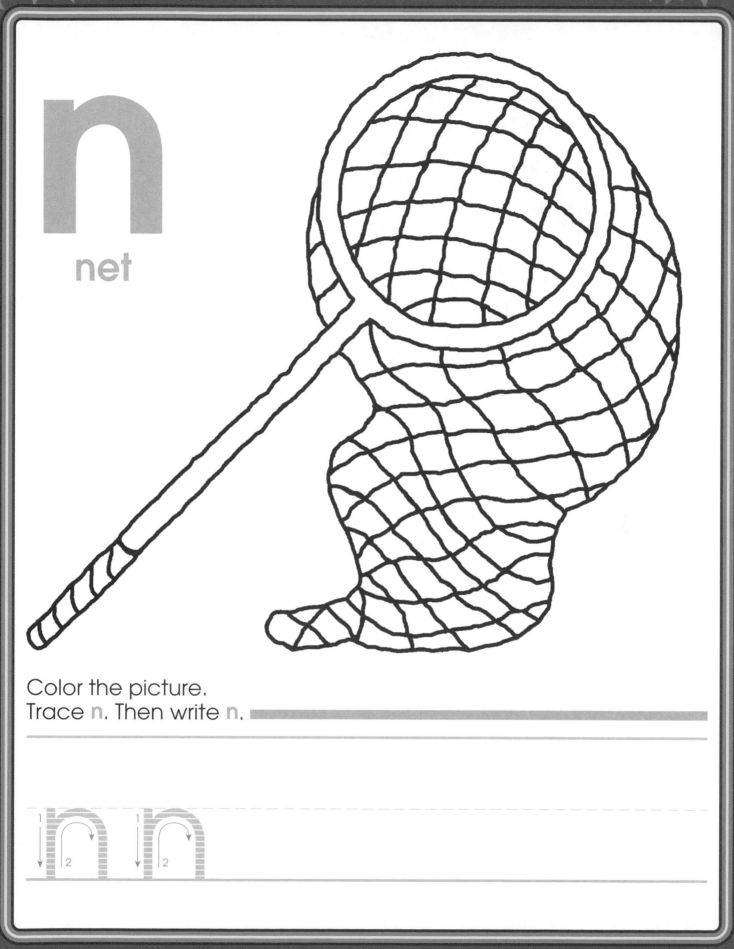

n

net

Color the picture.
Trace n. Then write n.

O

OSTRICH

Color the picture.
Trace **O**. Then write **O**.

o otter

Color the picture.
Trace **o**. Then write **o**.

Alphabet

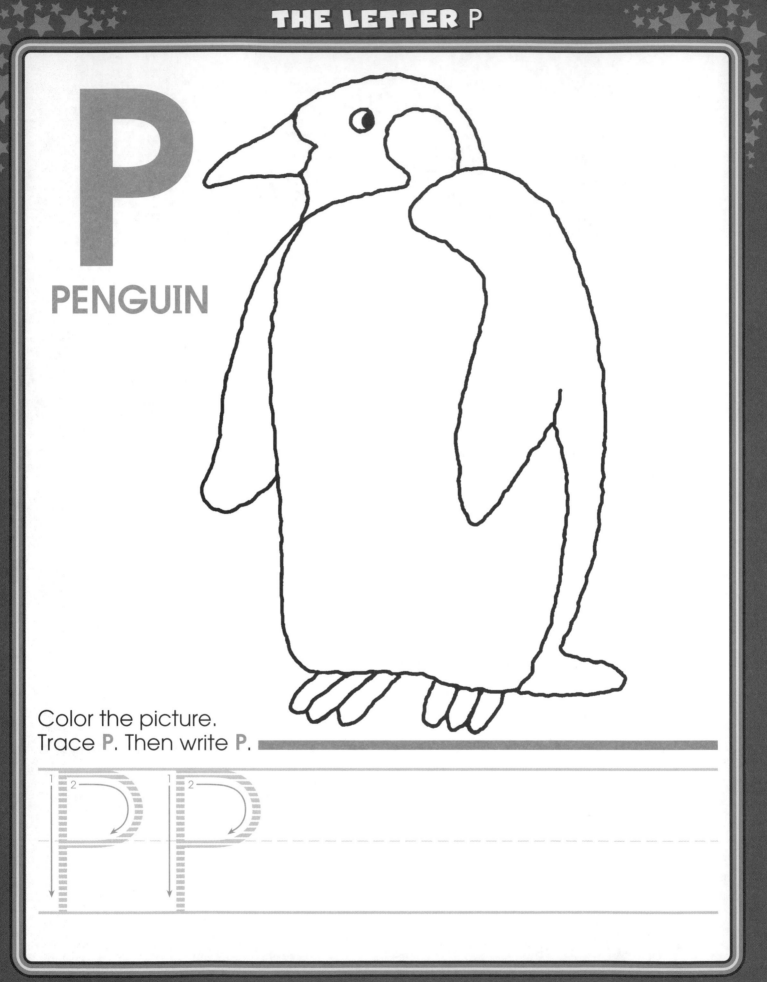

P

PENGUIN

Color the picture.
Trace P. Then write P.

p

pig

Color the picture.
Trace p. Then write p.

Q

QUARTER

UNITED STATES OF AMERICA

IN
GOD WE
TRUST

S

LIBERTY

QUARTER DOLLAR

Color the picture.
Trace Q. Then write Q.

quilt

Color the picture.
Trace **q**. Then write **q**.

R

RABBIT

Color the picture.
Trace **R**. Then write **R**.

r

raccoon

Color the picture.
Trace r. Then write r.

S
SEAL

Color the picture.
Trace S. Then write S.

S
sun

Color the picture.
Trace s. Then write s.

S S

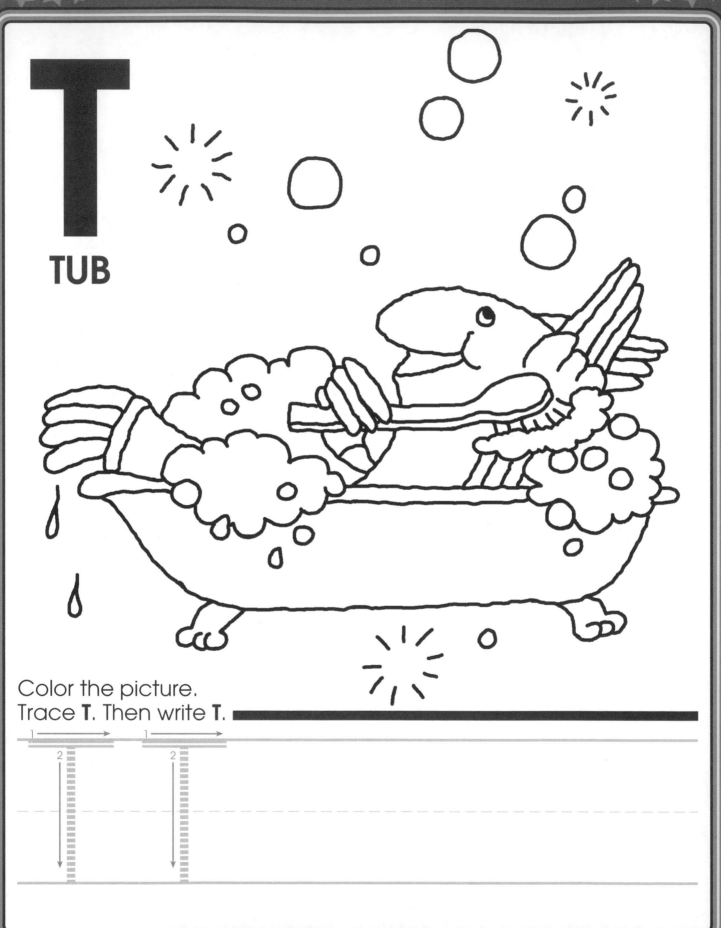

T
TUB

Color the picture.
Trace **T**. Then write **T**.

t

turtle

Color the picture.
Trace **t**. Then write **t**.

U

UMBRELLA

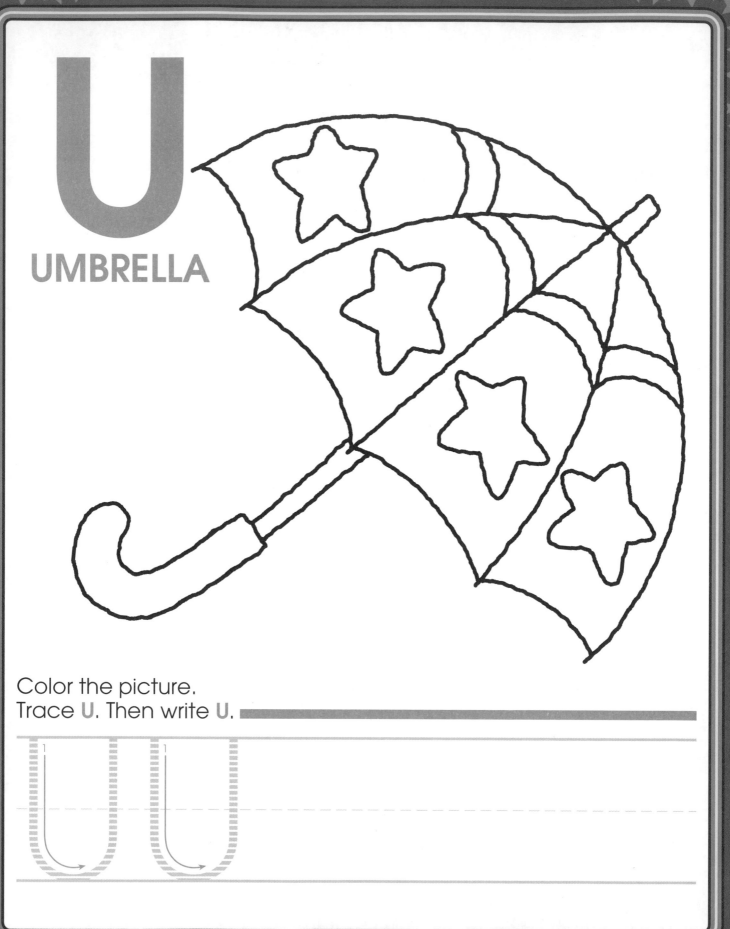

Color the picture.
Trace **U**. Then write **U**.

u

usher

Color the picture.
Trace **u**. Then write **u**.

Alphabet

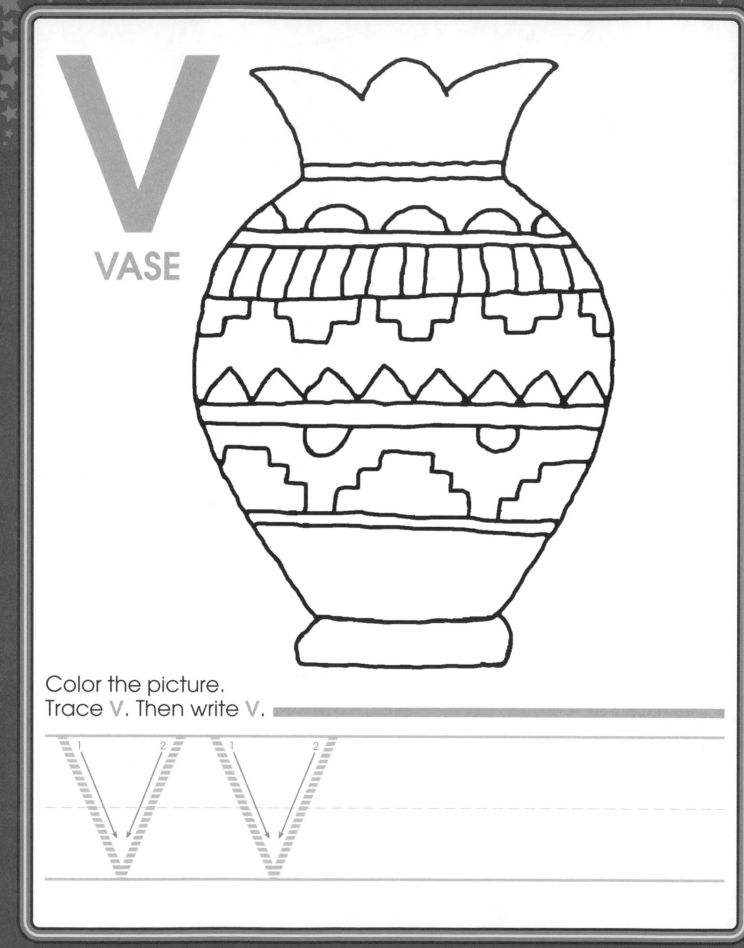

V

VASE

Color the picture.
Trace V. Then write V.

vet

Color the picture.
Trace **v**. Then write **v**.

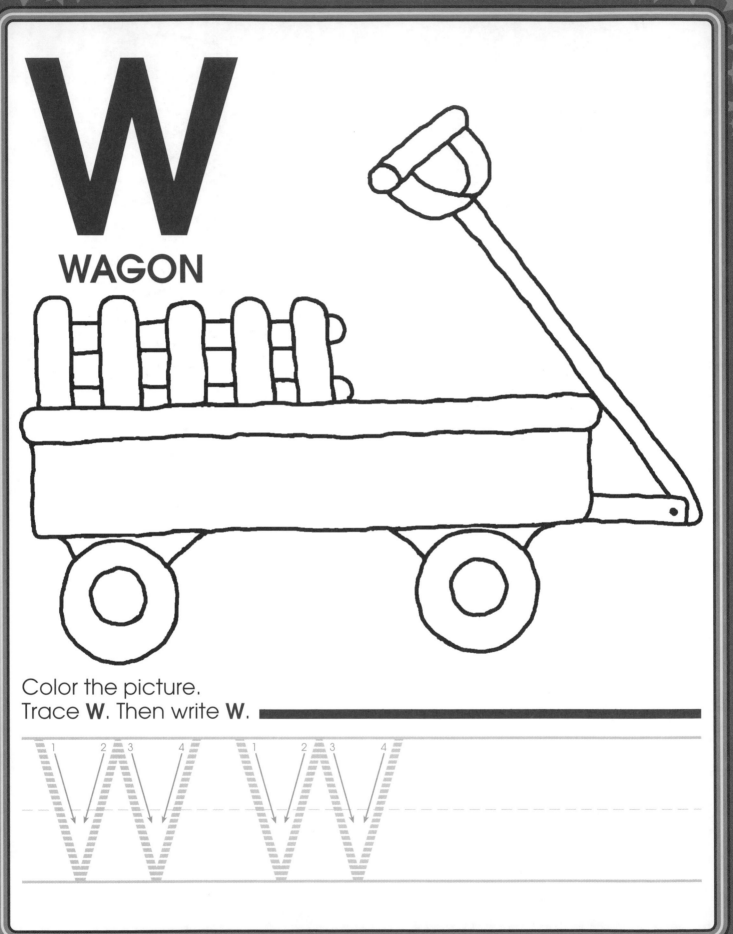

W

WAGON

Color the picture.
Trace **W**. Then write **W**.

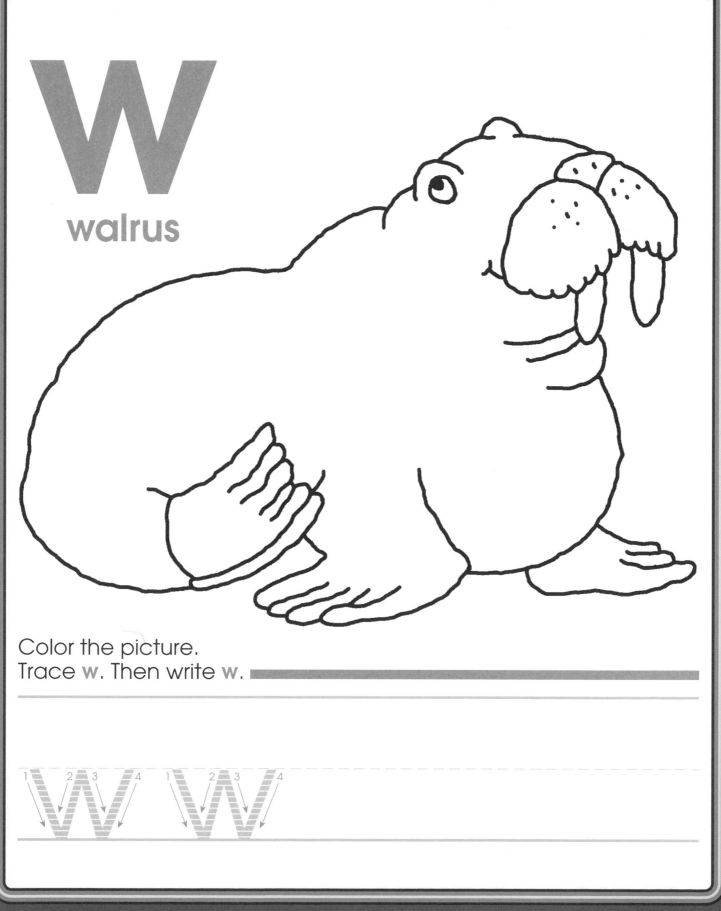

W

walrus

Color the picture.
Trace **w**. Then write **w**.

X

X marks the spot.

Color the picture.
Trace X. Then write X.

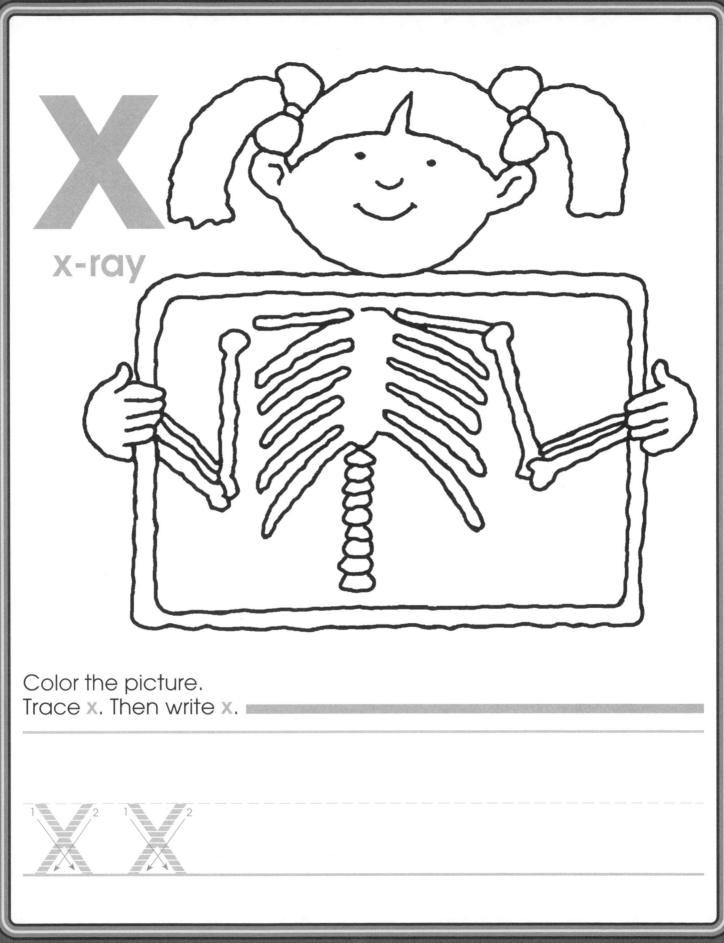

X
x-ray

Color the picture.
Trace x. Then write x.

Y

YAK

Color the picture.
Trace **Y**. Then write **Y**.

y

yo-yo

Color the picture.
Trace **y**. Then write **y**.

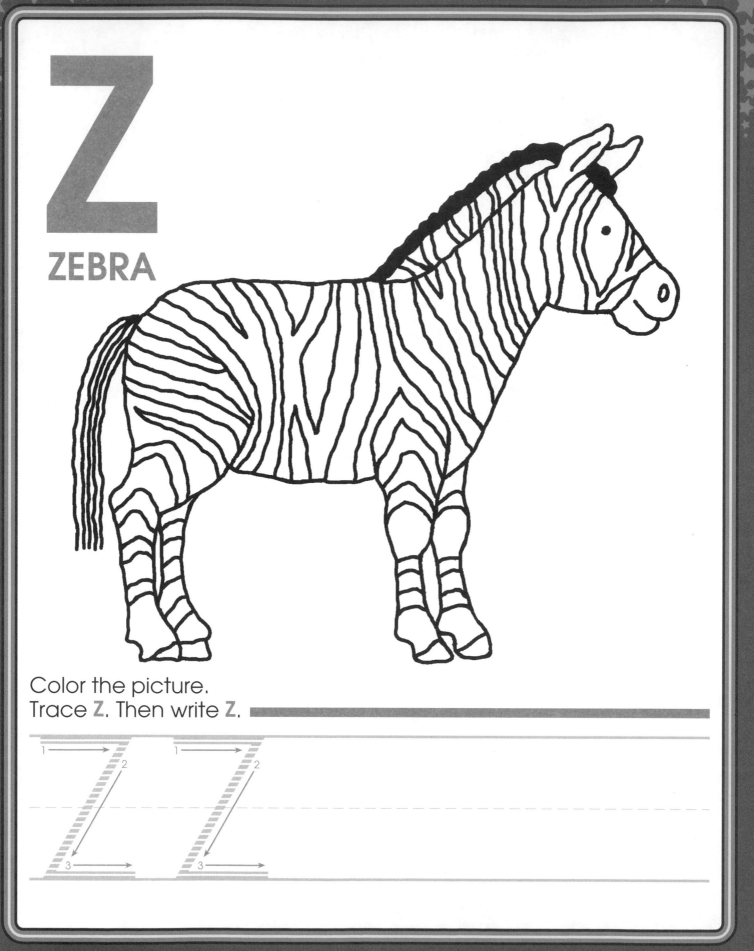

Z
ZEBRA

Color the picture.
Trace **Z**. Then write **Z**.

Z

ZOO

Color the picture.
Trace z. Then write z.

BEGINNING SOUNDS

Say each picture word.
Circle the letter that begins the word.

V
D
B
C

B
C
T
J

A
M
P
R

X
P
D
E

F
O
N
W

E
G
H
K

Say each picture word.
Circle the letter that begins the word.

Q A D F

O B Z C

B E M O

U Y G A

V H J I

N W L R

Alphabet

Say each picture word.
Circle the letter that begins the word.

B
P
U
G

A
V
W
U

S
P
R
C

W
Z
D
R

H
J
N
I

V
L
S
U

BEGINNING SOUNDS

Say each picture word.
Circle the letter that begins the word.

Write the letter that begins each picture word.

Write the letter that begins each picture word.

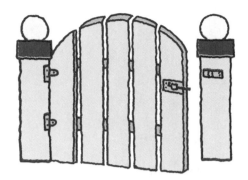

Write the letter that begins each picture word.

Write the letter that begins each picture word.

This section will teach your child to recognize the numbers 1-10 and count, which are important early math skills. Here are some tips to help your child get the most from this section:

- To help your child learn the numbers in numerical order, encourage your child to work from the beginning to the end of this section.

- The pages have both number names and numerals to ensure that your child will learn to recognize both. Encourage your child to say each number and count the playful illustrations that show each amount.

- The counting activities will help reinforce each number since your child will have to select the correct groups that show each number. Show your child how to count the objects by pointing to each object, one at a time.

- The writing component will help your child practice writing the numbers 1-10. The pages show the proper starting points for each stroke. Encourage your child to follow the arrows, which will help your child form the numbers correctly.

Circle 1 🦴.

1 ONE

There is 1 of something. Circle the 1 thing.

Trace 1. Then write 1.

Numbers

2 TWO

Circle 2  s.

There are **2** of something. Circle the group of **2**.

Trace **2**. Then write **2**.

Numbers

3
THREE

Circle 3 🌼 s.

There are **3** of something. Circle the group of **3**.

Trace **3**. Then write **3**.

4

FOUR

Circle **4** 🍦 s.

There are **4** of something. Circle the group of **4**.

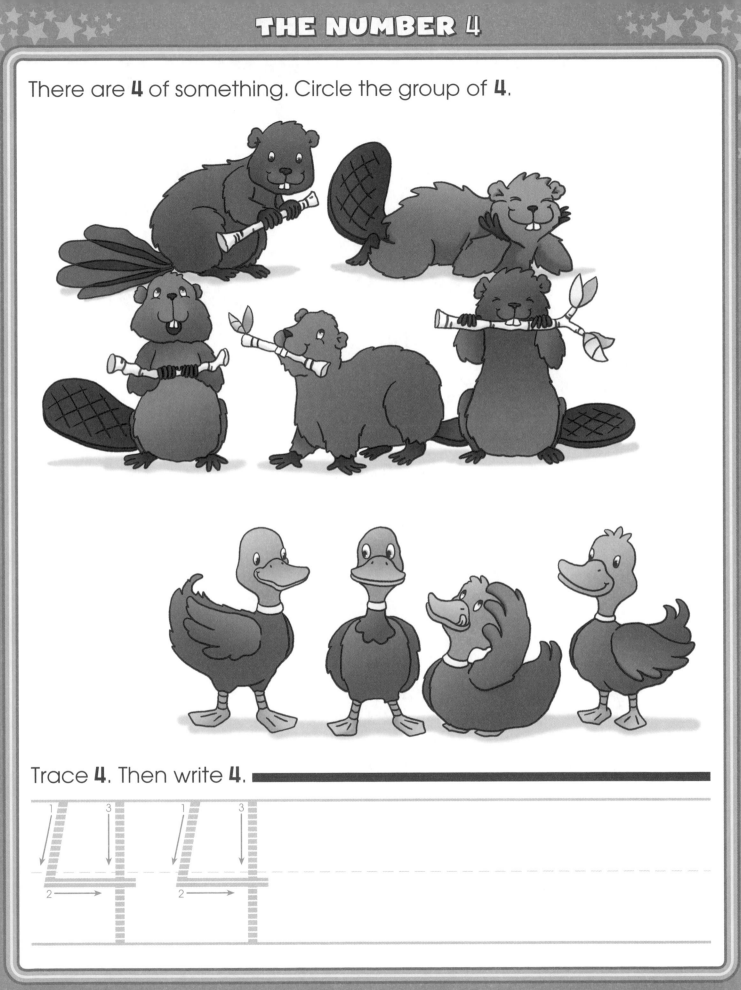

Trace **4**. Then write **4**.

5
FIVE

Circle 5 🚒 s.

There are 5 of something. Circle the group of 5.

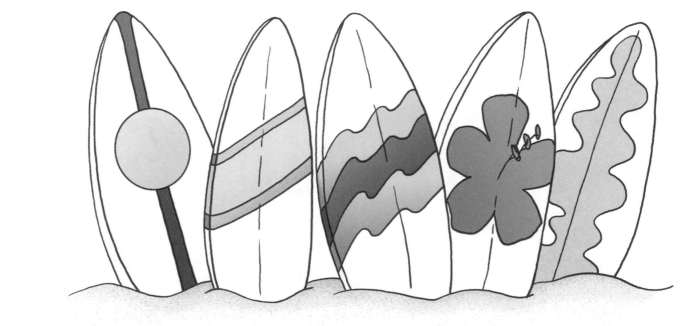

Trace 5. Then write 5.

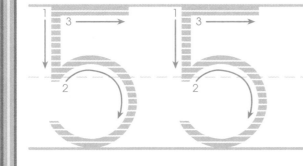

6
SIX

Circle 6 🪺 s.

There are **6** of something. Circle the group of **6**.

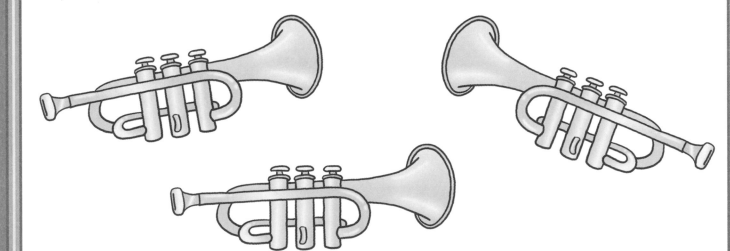

Trace **6**. Then write **6**.

7
SEVEN

Circle **7** 🌰 s.

There are **7** of something. Circle the group of **7**.

Trace **7**. Then write **7**.

Numbers

Circle 8  s.

8

EIGHT

There are **8** of something. Circle the group of **8**.

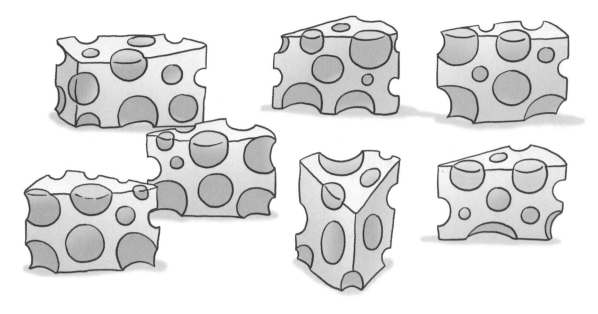

Trace **8**. Then write **8**.

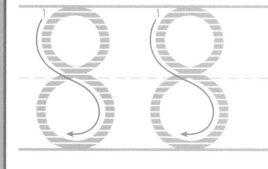

Numbers

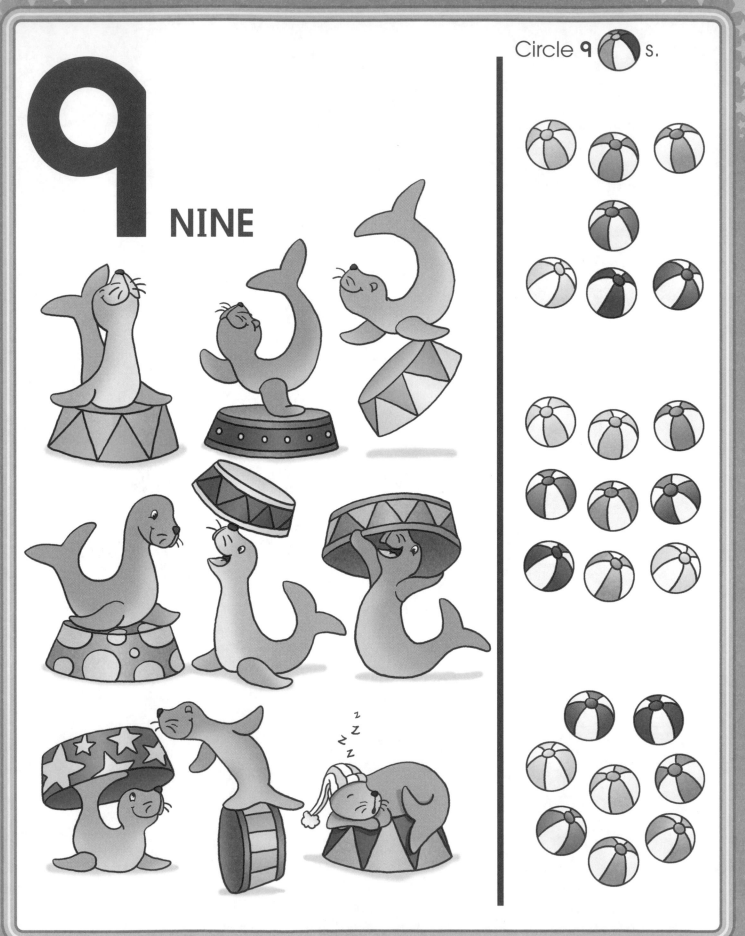

9 NINE

Circle 9 🏐 s.

There are **9** of something. Circle the group of **9**.

Trace **9**. Then write **9**.

Numbers

10
TEN

Circle 10 socks.

There are 10 of something. Circle the group of 10.

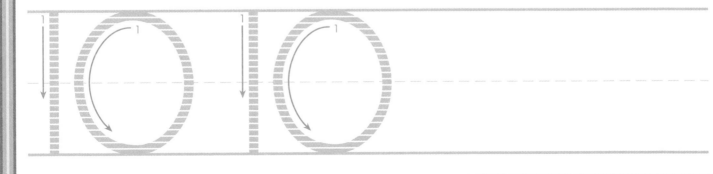

Trace 10. Then write 10.

Trace the number. Then write it.

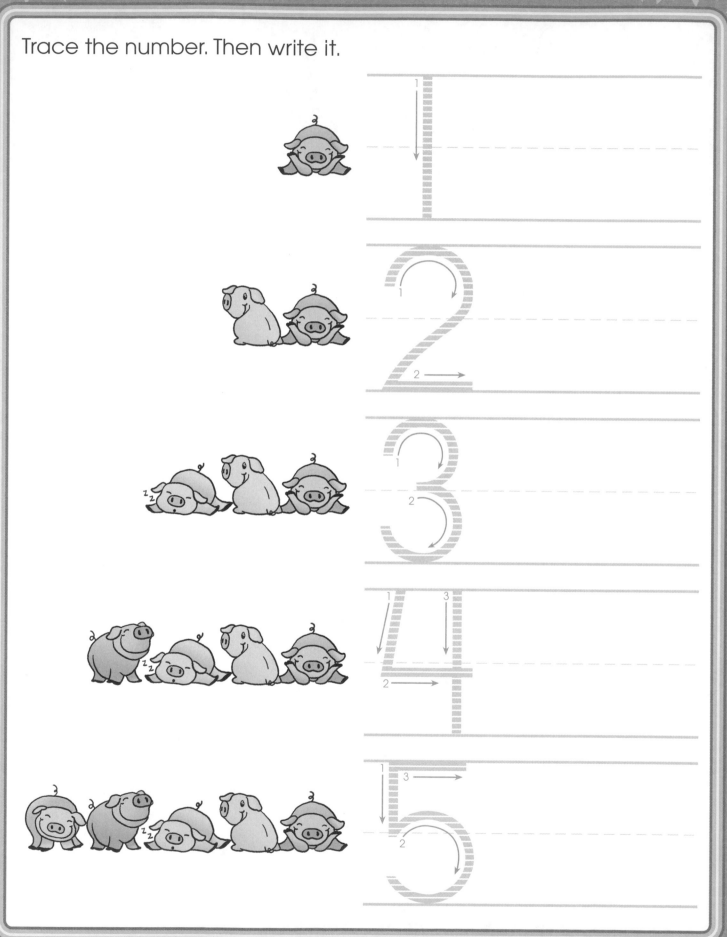

Trace the number. Then write it.

This section focuses on learning to recognize and identify colors and basic shapes. The section is divided into two parts:

- The shape portion features a variety of activities that introduce the names and characteristics of circles, squares, triangles, rectangles, and ovals.

- The color portion features an assortment of activities that will teach your child to identify colors and write color words.

This is a **circle**.

Circle the **2** ⬭ shapes.

Color the ◯.

Color the **2** ◯ shapes.

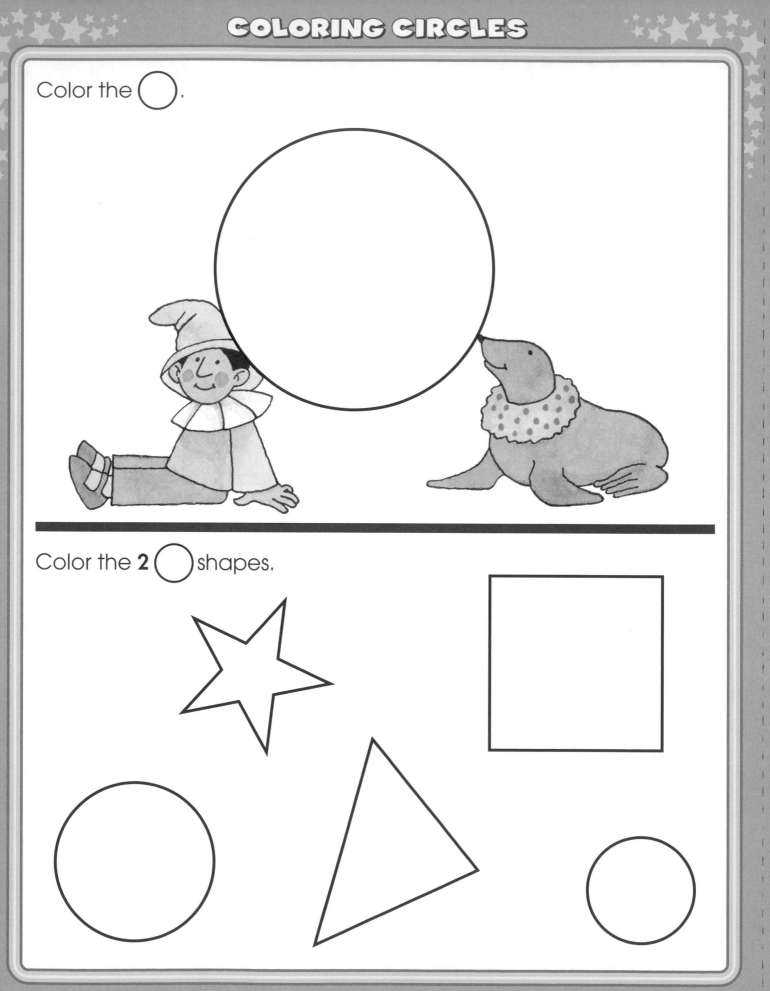

Color the ⬭ orange.

Trace the ◯s.

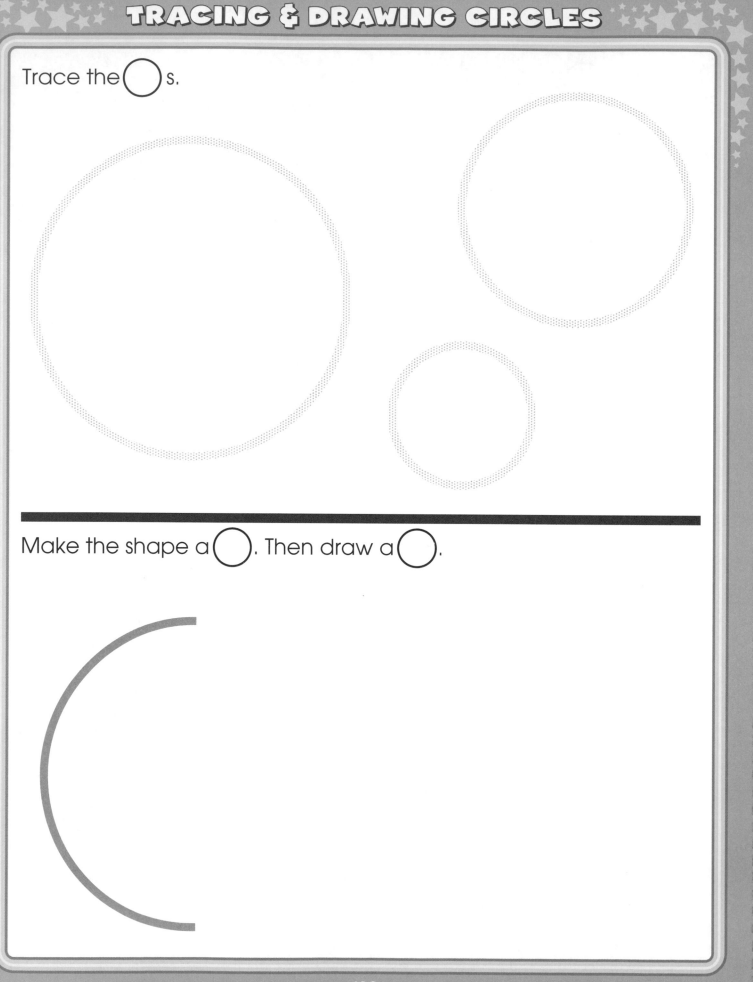

Make the shape a ◯. Then draw a ◯.

Circle the ◯ shapes in the picture.

How many ◯s did you find? _____

Shapes & Colors

This is a **square**.

Circle the **2** ☐ shapes.

Color the ☐ .

Color the **2** ☐ shapes.

125

Shapes & Colors

Color the ⬜ **red**.

Trace the ☐ s.

Make the shape a ☐. Then draw a ☐.

SQUARE SEARCH

Circle the ☐ shapes in the picture.

How many ☐s did you find? _____

This is a **triangle**.

Circle the **2**  shapes.

Color the △.

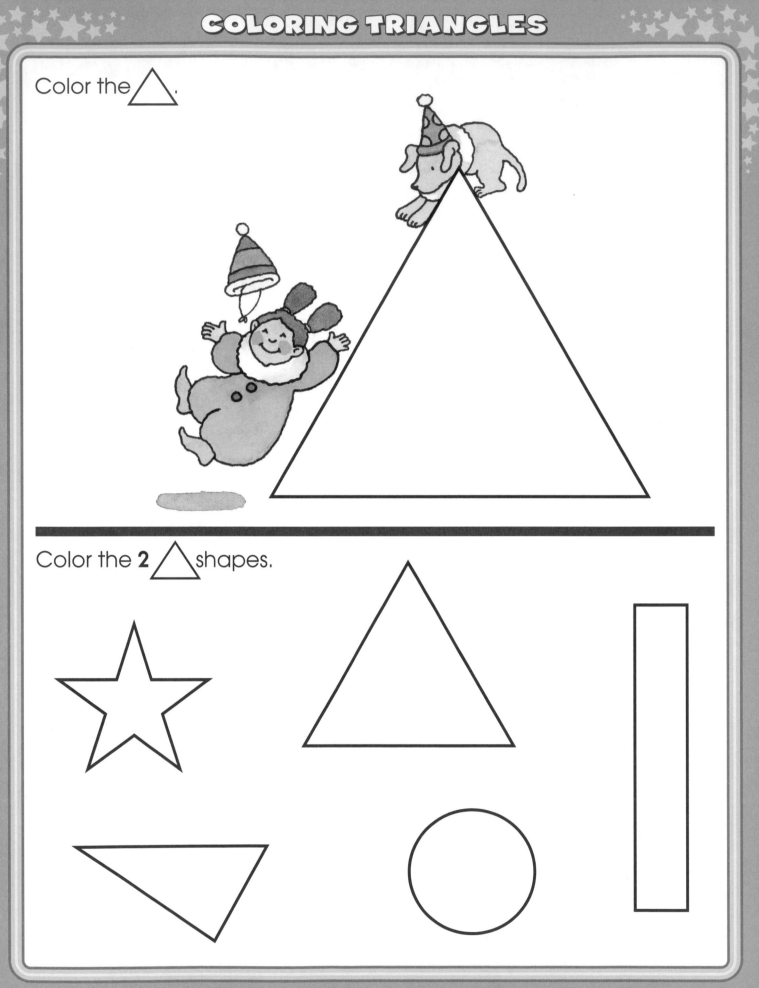

Color the 2 △ shapes.

Color the △ yellow.

Shapes & Colors

Trace the △s.

Make the shape a △. Then draw a △.

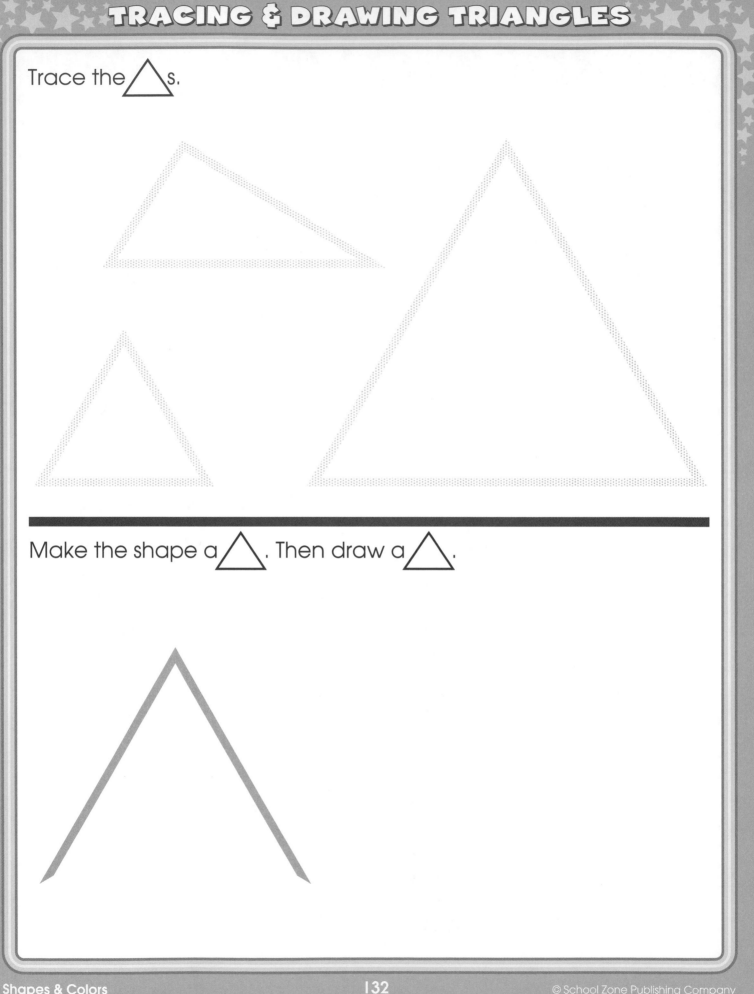

Circle the △ shapes in the picture.

How many △s did you find? _____

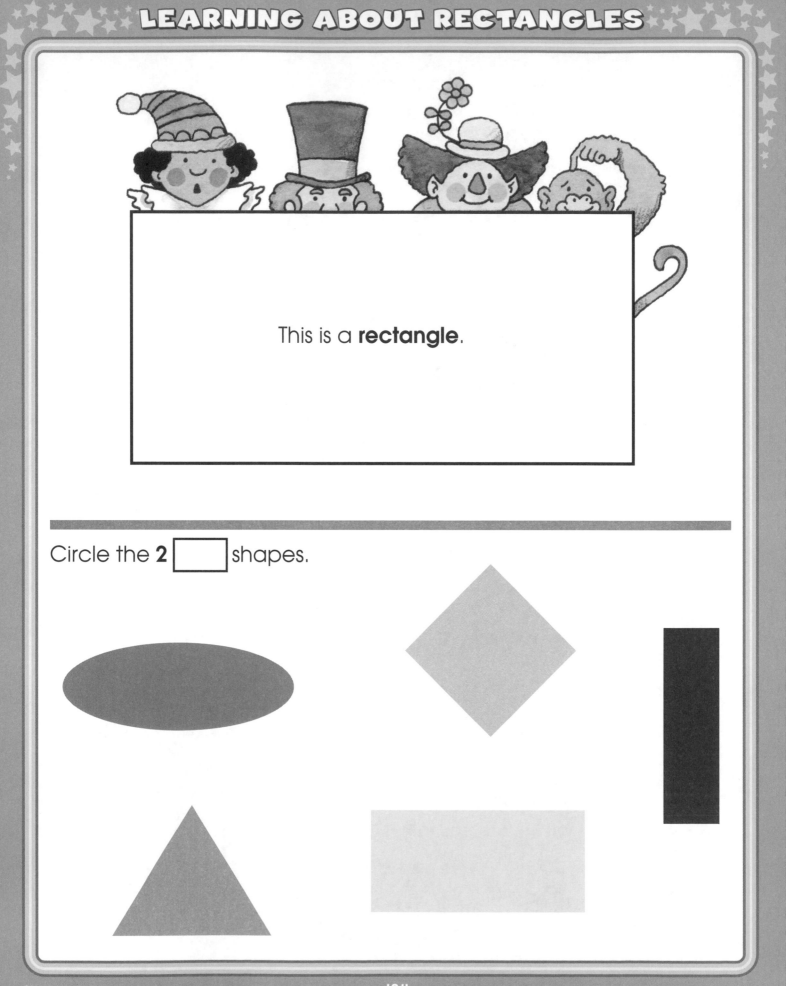

This is a **rectangle**.

Circle the **2** ☐ shapes.

Color the ⬜ .

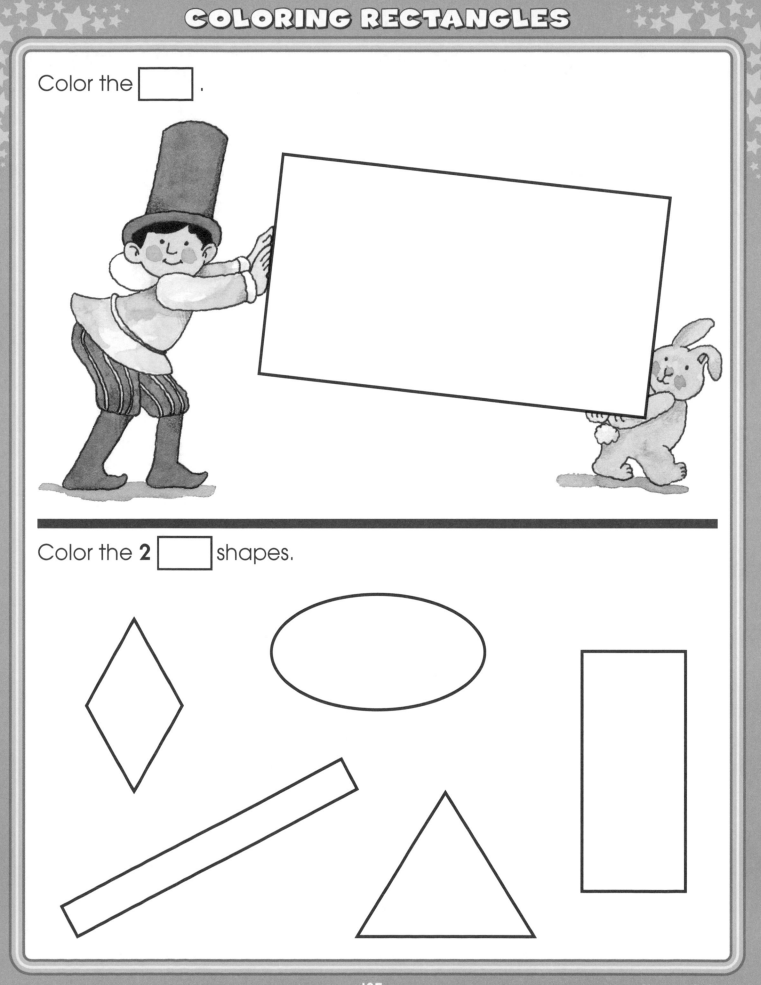

Color the **2** ⬜ shapes.

Color the ☐ green.

Trace the ▭ s.

Make the shape a ▭. Then draw a ▭.

RECTANGLE SEARCH

Circle the ☐ shapes in the picture.

How many ☐s did you find? _____

This is an **oval**.

Circle the **2** ⬭ shapes.

Color the 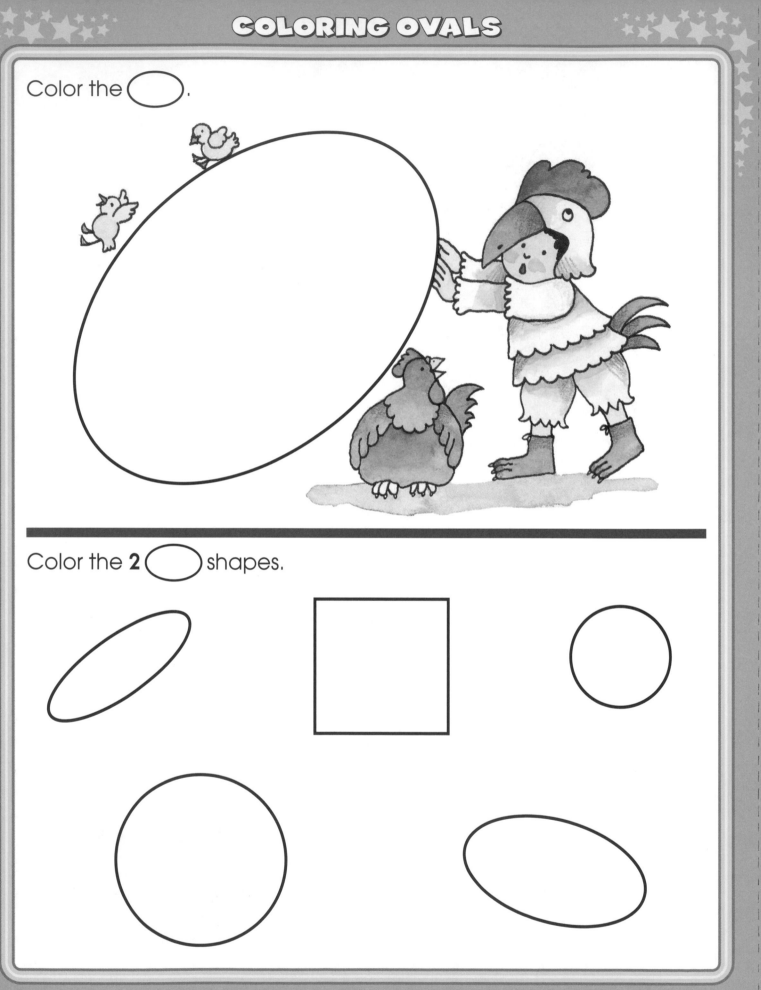.

Color the **2** ⬭ shapes.

Color the ⬭ blue.

Trace the ⬭s.

Make the shape an ⬭. Then draw an ⬭.

Circle the ⬭ shapes in the picture.

How many ⬭s did you find? _____

Draw a line between the shapes that have the same name.

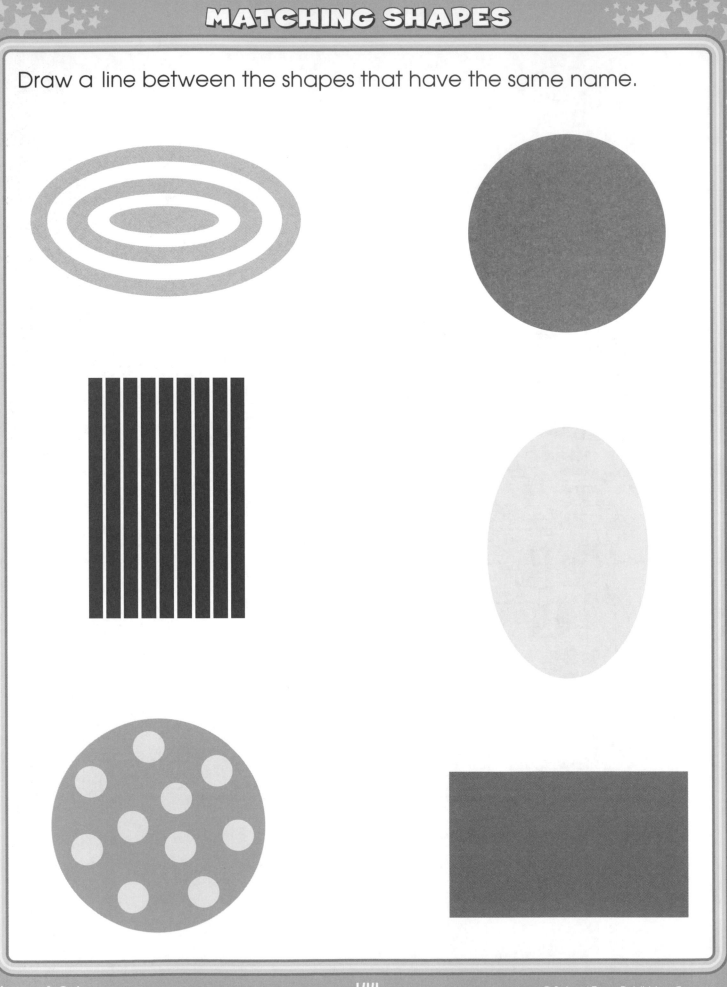

Draw a line between the shapes that have the same name.

Shapes & Colors

Color all the ◯s **purple**.

Color all the ▭s **red**.

Color all the △s yellow.

Color all the ▭s green.

Shapes & Colors

Color all the ◯s orange.

Color all the ▢s blue.

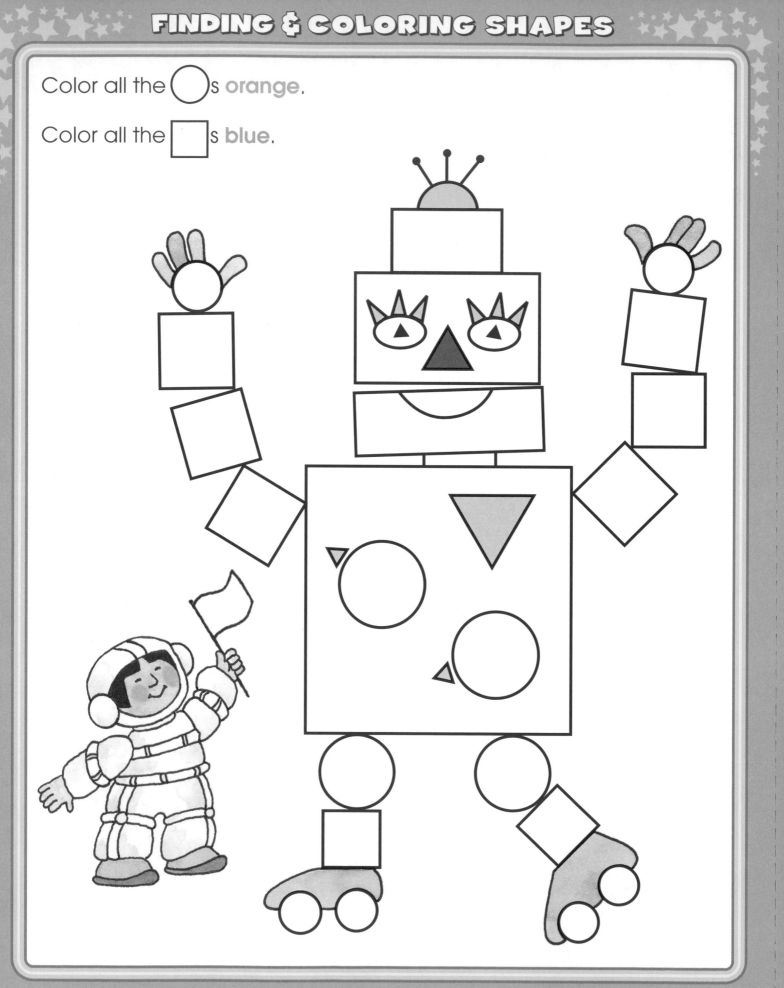

Trace the ☐ . Then draw a ☐ .

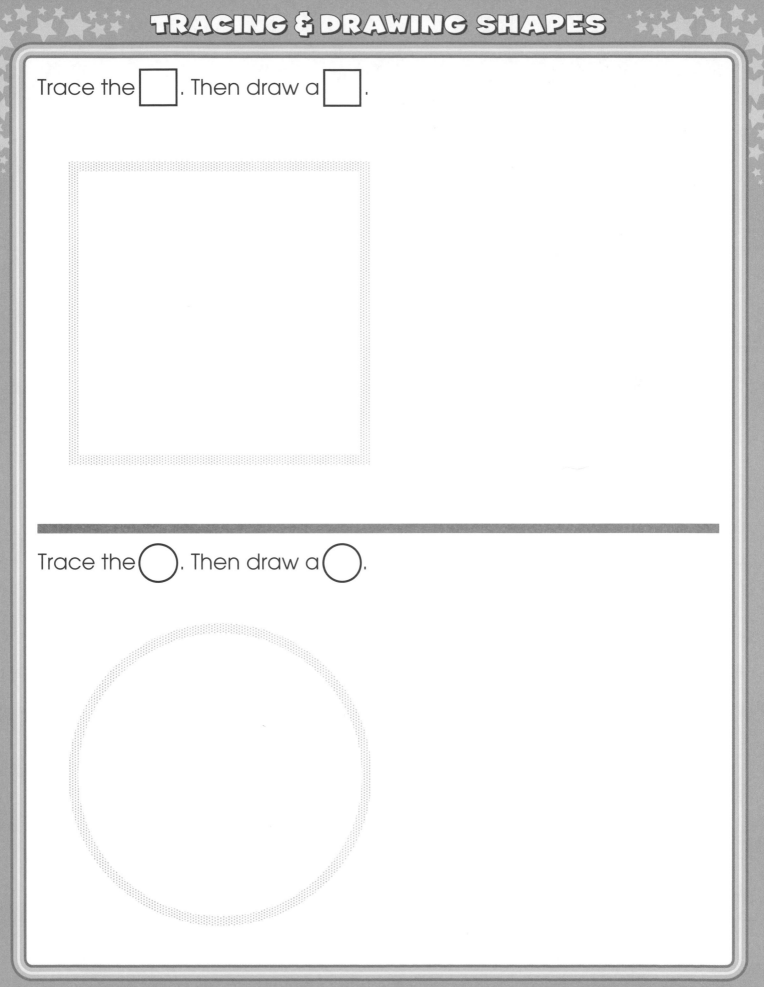

Trace the ◯ . Then draw a ◯ .

Trace the △. Then draw a △.

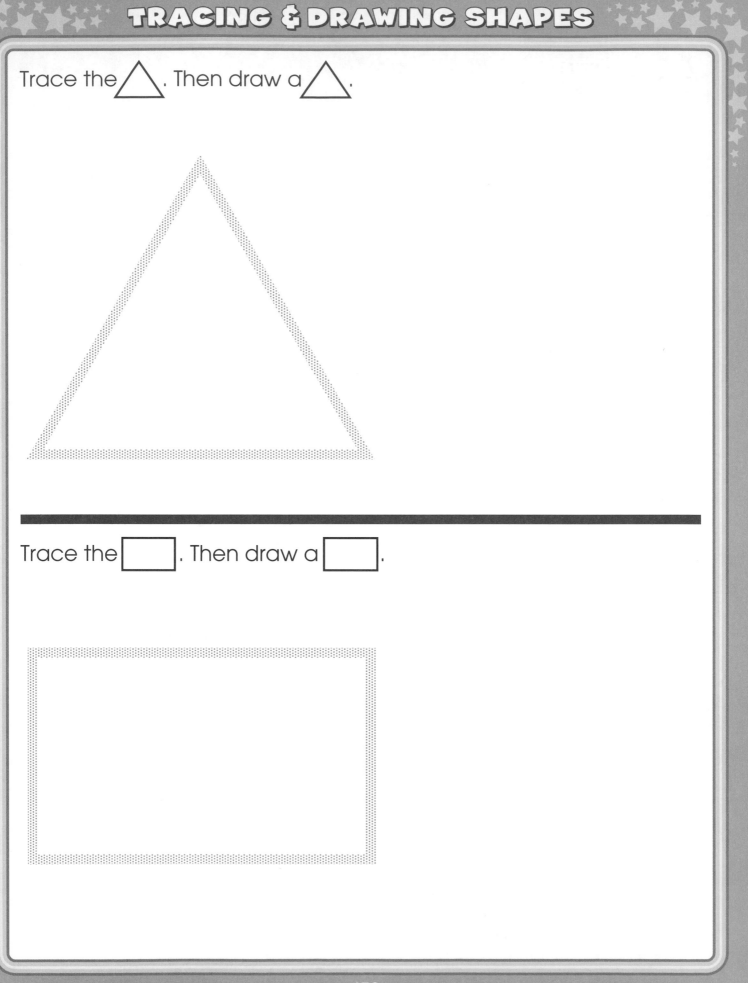

Trace the ▭. Then draw a ▭.

Color the  red.

Use your ✏ to trace the word **red**.

red

Color what is **red**.

Color the  red.

Circle **2** things that are **red**.

Shapes & Colors

Color the 🍎 **purple**.

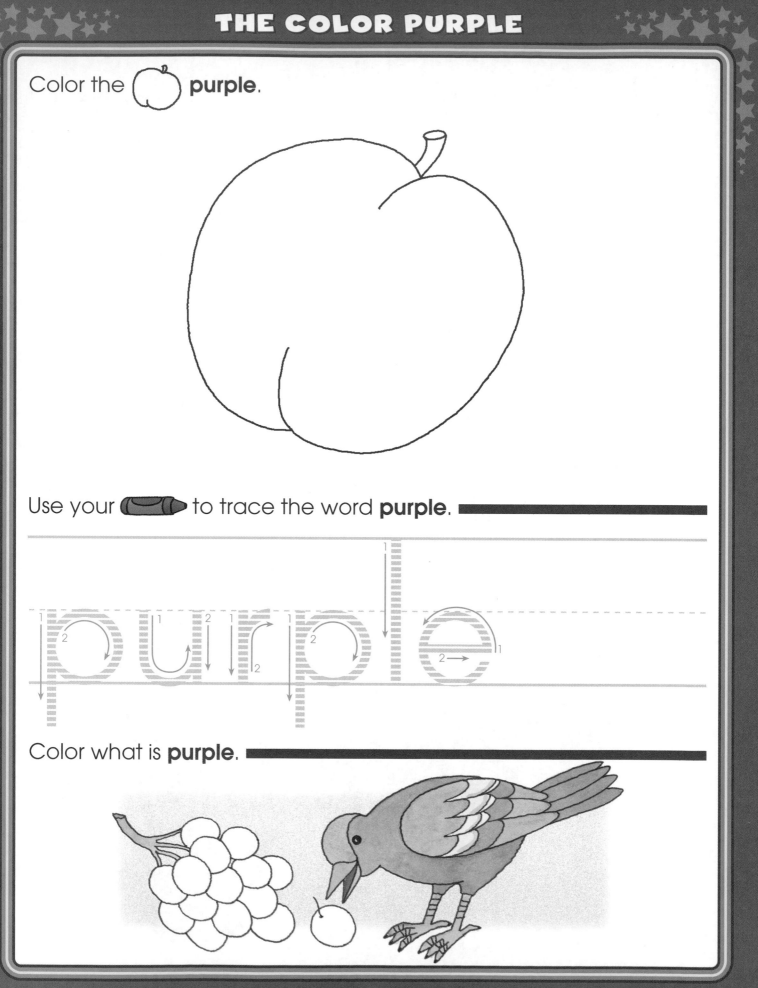

Use your ✏️ to trace the word **purple**.

purple

Color what is **purple**.

THE COLOR PURPLE

Color the king's  purple.

Circle **3** things that are **purple**.

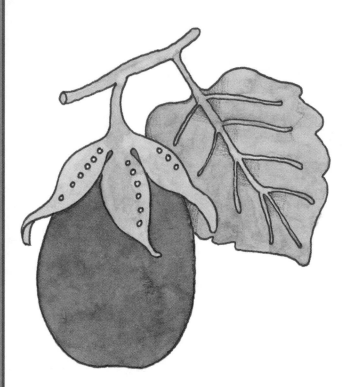

Color the 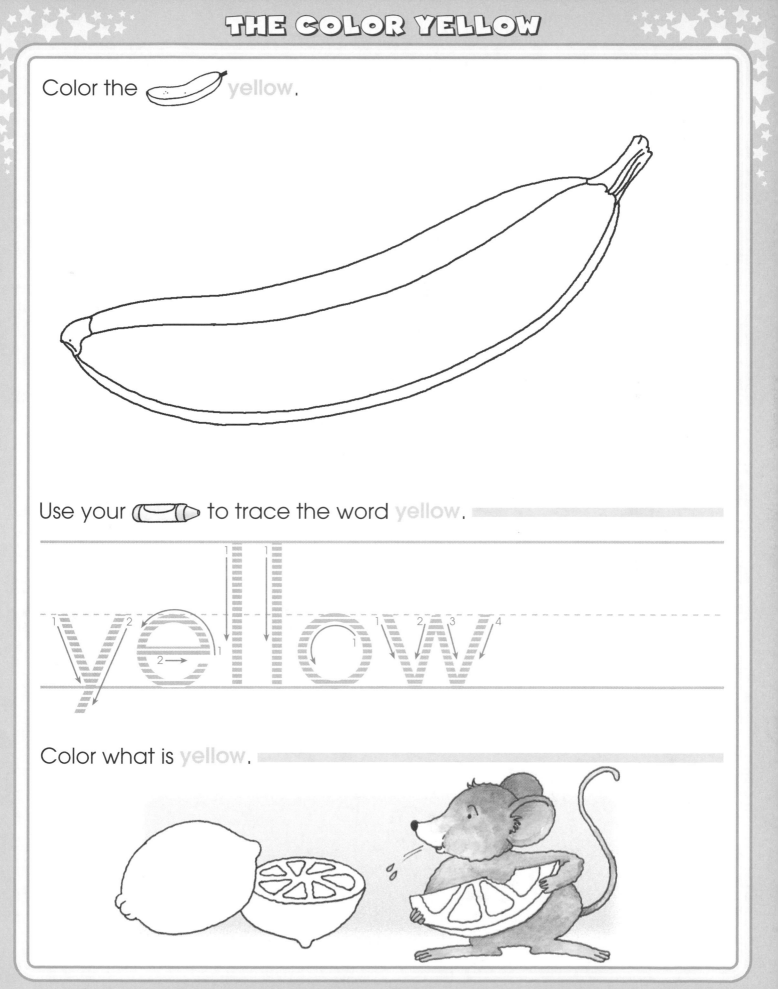 yellow.

Use your ✏ to trace the word yellow.

yellow

Color what is yellow.

Color the  yellow.

Circle 3 things that are yellow.

Shapes & Colors

Color the 🫐 blue.

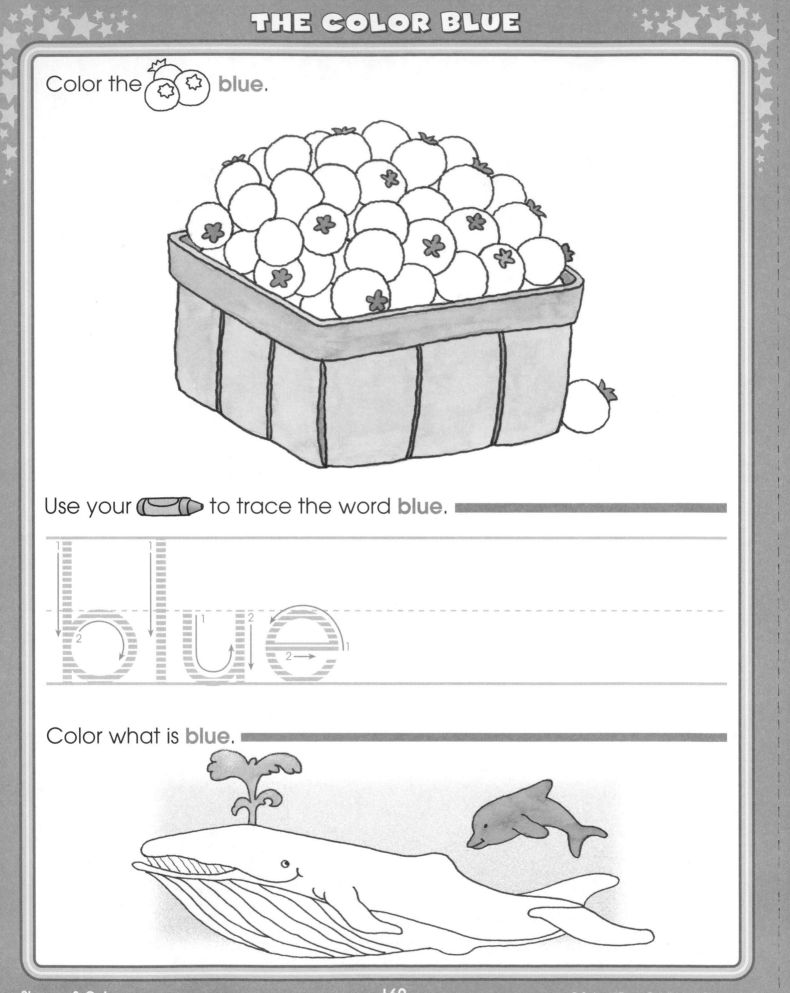

Use your ✏️ to trace the word **blue**.

blue

Color what is **blue**.

Color the  blue.

Circle **3** things that are **blue**.

Color the  brown.

Use your  to trace the word **brown**.

Color what is **brown**.

Shapes & Colors

Color the  **brown**.

164

Circle **2** things that are **brown**.

Color the 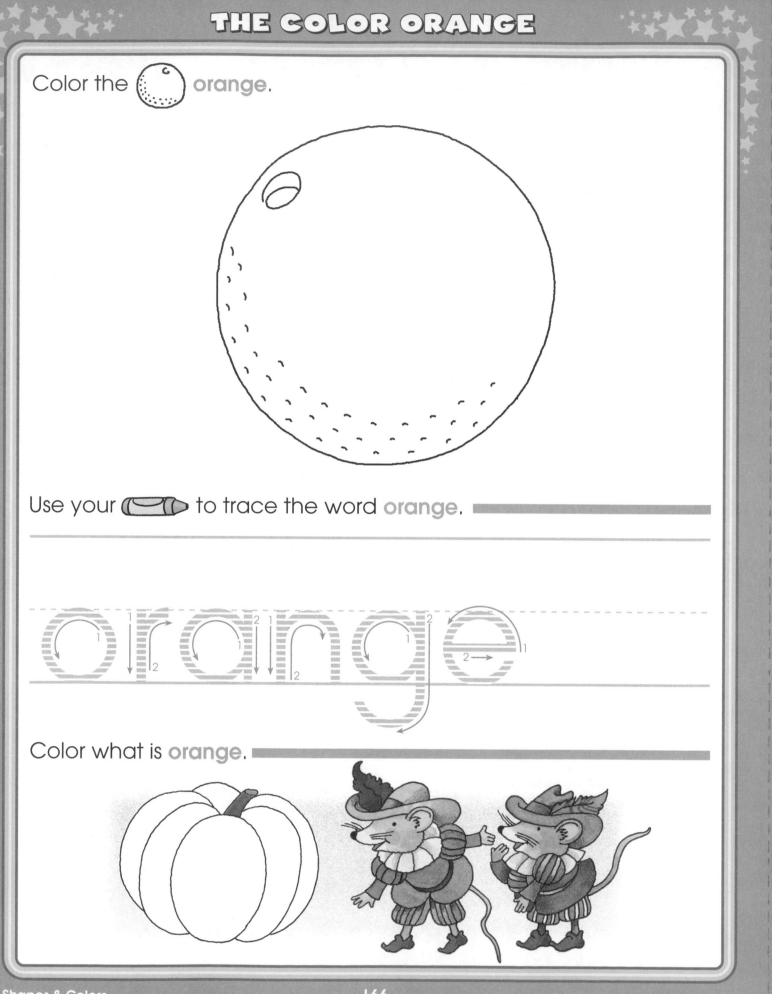 orange.

Use your ✏ to trace the word orange.

orange

Color what is orange.

Color the  orange.

Circle 2 things that are orange.

Color the 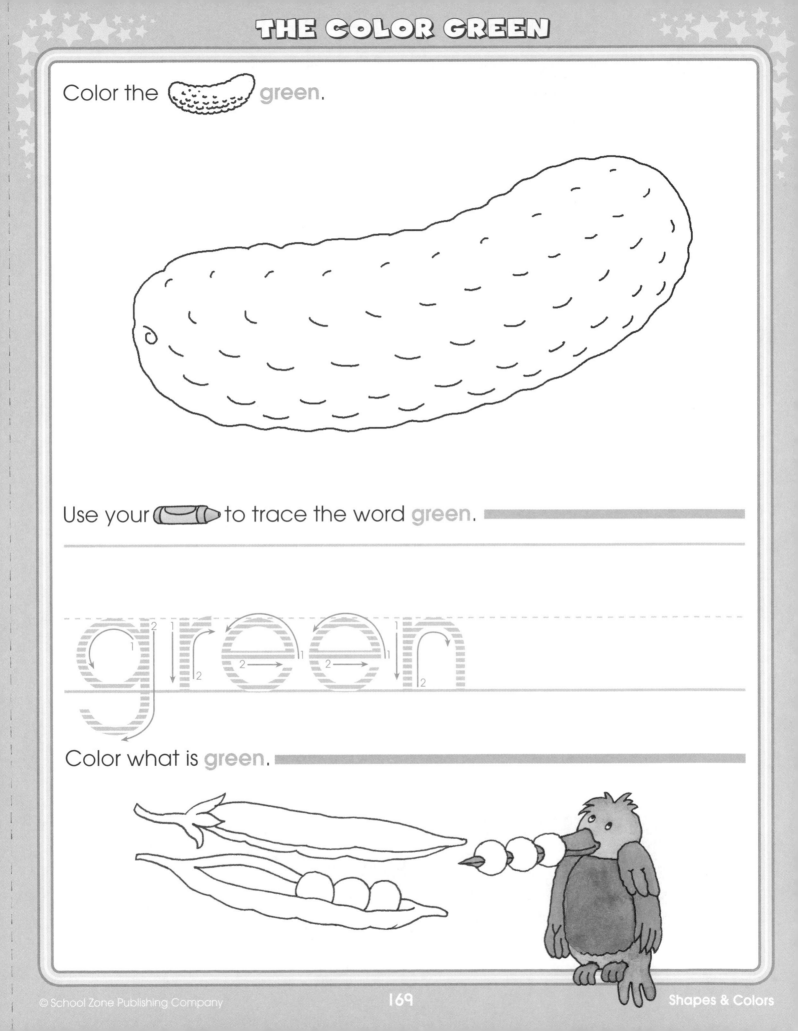 green.

Use your ▭ to trace the word green.

green

Color what is green.

Color the  green.

Circle **3** things that are **green**.

Color the  **black**.

Use your ▬ to trace the word **black**.

black

Color what is **black**.

Color the s **black**.

THE COLOR BLACK

Circle **2** things that are **black**.

Color the s **orange**. Color the **black**.

Shapes & Colors

Color the  green. Color the red.

Color the  **blue**. Color the ⚪ yellow.

Color the  yellow. Color the purple.

Color the  **brown**. Color the 🔴 **red**.

Draw a line from each crayon to the picture that is usually that color. Color the pictures.

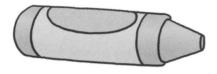

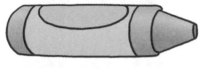

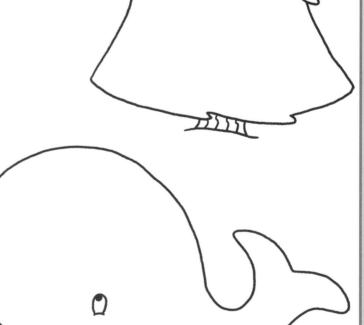

Draw a line from each crayon to the picture that is usually that color. Color the pictures.

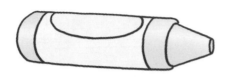
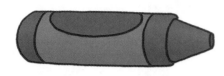
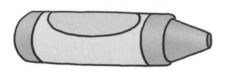

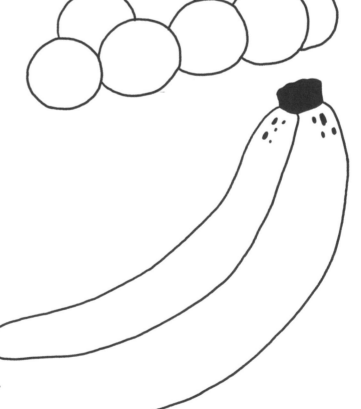

#

Learning to recognize the sounds letters make is an essential early reading skill. Here are some tips to help your child get the most from this section:

- Encourage your child to say each letter and pronounce the word for each picture. This will help your child learn to recognize the sounds of letters.

- If your child is having trouble identifying which sounds are the same, encourage him or her to say the words again and to sound out each word carefully.

- To help your child identify the beginning and ending sounds of words, encourage your child to say each word slowly to hear the sounds.

Circle the **2** pictures that begin with the **T** sound.

T

TURTLE

Phonics

Circle the **2** pictures that begin with the **M** sound.

M
MONKEYS

Circle the **2** pictures that begin with the **B** sound.

B
BICYCLE

Circle the **2** pictures that begin with the **S** sound.

S
SEALS

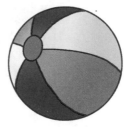

Circle the picture that **begins** with the **same sound** as the first one.

Say the picture word.
Circle the picture that **begins** with the **same sound** as the first one.

T tomato

M mushroom

B boy

S sandwich

TRY IT!

Draw a large boat. Write A, B, C, and D on the boat. Cut out pictures of things that begin with each of the letters, and then glue the pictures to the boat.

Circle the **2** pictures that begin with the **P** sound.

P
PIGS

Circle the **2** pictures that begin with the **L** sound.

L
LEAVES

Circle the **2** pictures that begin with the **N** sound.

N
NUTS

Circle the **2** pictures that begin with the **D** sound.

D
DOG

BEGINNING SOUNDS

Circle the picture that **begins** with the **same sound** as the first one.

Say the picture word.
Circle the picture that **begins** with the **same sound** as the first one.

P
penguin

L
lion

N
newspaper

D
dress

TRY IT!

Play animal alphabet with a friend. Name an animal and ask your friend to think of something else that begins with the same letter as the animal's name.

Circle the **2** pictures that begin with the **F** sound.

F

FISH

Circle the **2** pictures that begin with the **H** sound.

H
HAT

Circle the **2** pictures that begin with the **R** sound.

R
ROOSTER

Phonics

Circle the **2** pictures that begin with the **J** sound.

J

JET

BEGINNING SOUNDS

Circle the picture that **begins** with the **same sound** as the first one.

Say the picture word.
Circle the picture that **begins** with the **same sound** as the first one.

F
fox

H
hamburger

R
ring

J
jacket

TRY IT!

Think of words that start with each letter of the alphabet to make up silly animal descriptions. For instance, "giddy goose", "messy mouse", or "purple, picky pig".

Circle the **2** pictures that begin with the **K** sound.

K
KANGAROOS

Phonics

Circle the **2** pictures that begin with the **W** sound.

Circle the **2** pictures that begin with the **Y** sound.

Y
YAK

Phonics

Circle the **2** pictures that begin with the **V** sound.

V

VALENTINES

Be Mine

BEGINNING SOUNDS

Circle the picture that **begins** with the **same sound** as the first one.

Say the picture word.
Circle the picture that **begins** with the **same sound** as the first one.

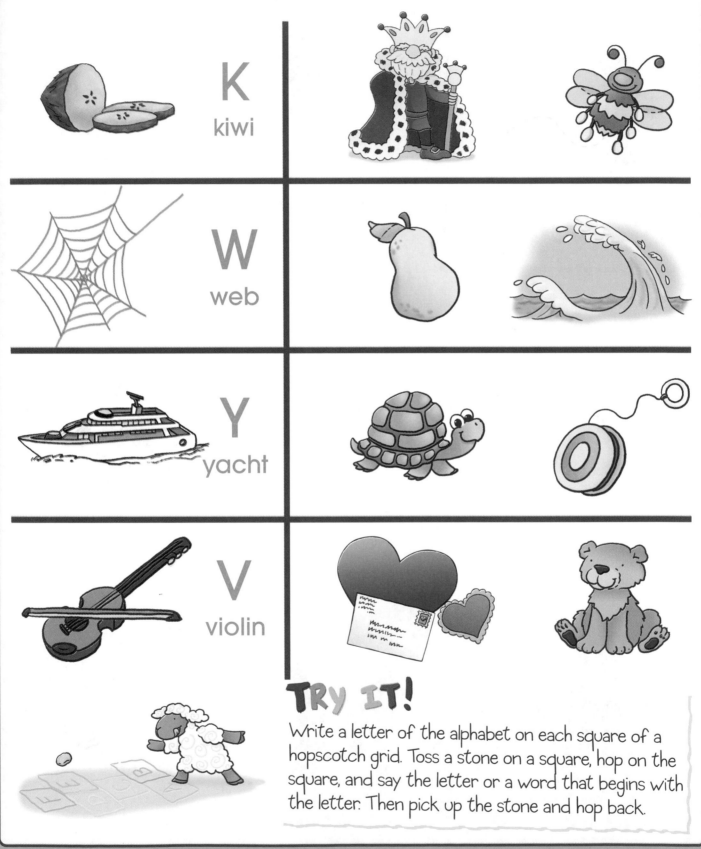

TRY IT!

Write a letter of the alphabet on each square of a hopscotch grid. Toss a stone on a square, hop on the square, and say the letter or a word that begins with the letter. Then pick up the stone and hop back.

Circle the **2** pictures that begin with the **Z** sound.

Z

ZOO

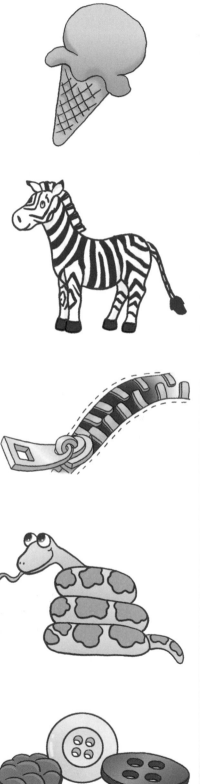

Phonics

Circle the **2** pictures that begin with the **Q** sound.

Q

QUEEN

Circle the **2** pictures that begin with the **C** sound.

C

COW

Phonics

Circle the **2** pictures that begin with the **G** sound.

G

GATE

Circle the picture that **begins** with the **same sound** as the first one.

BEGINNING SOUNDS

Say the picture word.
Circle the picture that **begins** with the **same sound** as the first one.

Z zero

Q quilt

C cat

G girl

TRY IT!

Go on an alphabet hunt! Pick a letter of the alphabet. Then look in an old newspaper or magazine to find names that begin with the letter. Circle the names with a marker or crayon.

Circle the **2** pictures that begin with the **A** sound.

A
ALLIGATOR

Phonics

Circle the **2** pictures that begin with the **E** sound.

E
ELEPHANT

Circle the **2** pictures that begin with the **I** sound.

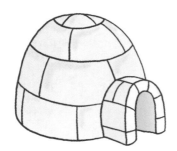

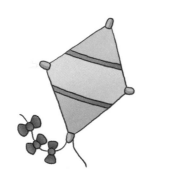

I

IGUANA

Phonics

Circle the **2** pictures that begin with the **O** sound.

O
OTTER

Circle the **2** pictures that begin with the **U** sound.

U
UMPIRE

BEGINNING SOUNDS

Circle the picture that **begins** with the **same sound** as the first one.

BEGINNING SOUNDS

Say the picture word.
Circle the picture that **begins** with the **same sound** as the first one.

A astronaut

E eye

I insects

O ox

U umpire

Say the name of the picture.
Circle the letter that is the **beginning sound** of the picture.

R   B

T   F

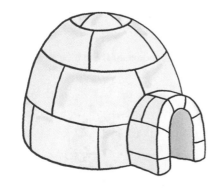

A   I

U   Q

Say the name of the picture.
Circle the letter that is the **beginning sound** of the picture.

B   V

G   A

N   M

Z   D

Say the name of the picture.
Circle the letter that is the **beginning sound** of the picture.

N   C

D   E

M   P

Y   T

Say the name of the picture.
Circle the letter that is the **beginning sound** of the picture.

G   B

L   M

P   R

D   S

Say the name of the picture.
Circle the letter that is the **beginning sound** of the picture.

U   W

Y   T

Q   R

B   E

Say the name of the picture.
Circle the letter that is the **beginning sound** of the picture.

C   N

H   L

J   K

K   B

Say the name of each picture.
Draw lines from each letter to the pictures that start with that sound.
Circle the picture that does not belong.

Say the name of each picture.
Draw lines from each letter to the pictures that start with that sound.
Circle the picture that does not belong.

BEGINNING SOUNDS

Say the name of each picture.
Draw lines from each letter to the pictures that start with that sound.
Circle the picture that does not belong.

Say the name of each picture.
Draw lines from each letter to the pictures that start with that sound.
Circle the picture that does not belong.

U

Y

Say the name of each picture.
Draw lines from each letter to the pictures that start with that sound.
Circle the picture that does not belong.

Say the name of each picture.
Draw lines from each letter to the pictures that start with that sound.
Circle the picture that does not belong.

Say the name of each picture.
Draw lines from each letter to the pictures that start with that sound.
Circle the picture that does not belong.

Say the name of each picture.
Draw lines from each letter to the pictures that start with that sound.
Circle the picture that does not belong.

Say the name of each picture.
Draw lines from each letter to the pictures that start with that sound.
Circle the picture that does not belong.

Say the name of each picture.
Draw lines from each letter to the pictures that start with that sound.
Circle the picture that does not belong.

R

O

K

Phonics

Say the name of each picture.
Draw lines from each letter to the pictures that start with that sound.
Circle the picture that does not belong.

Say the name of each picture.
Draw lines from each letter to the pictures that start with that sound.
Circle the picture that does not belong.

Say the name of the picture.
Write the letter that begins the word.

K M R H

____ AT

____ ITE

____ OON

____ ING

Say the name of the picture.
Write the letter that begins the word.

G N Y S

____OAT

____INE

____TAR

____ELLOW

Say the name of the picture.
Write the letter that begins the word.

D L   B Q

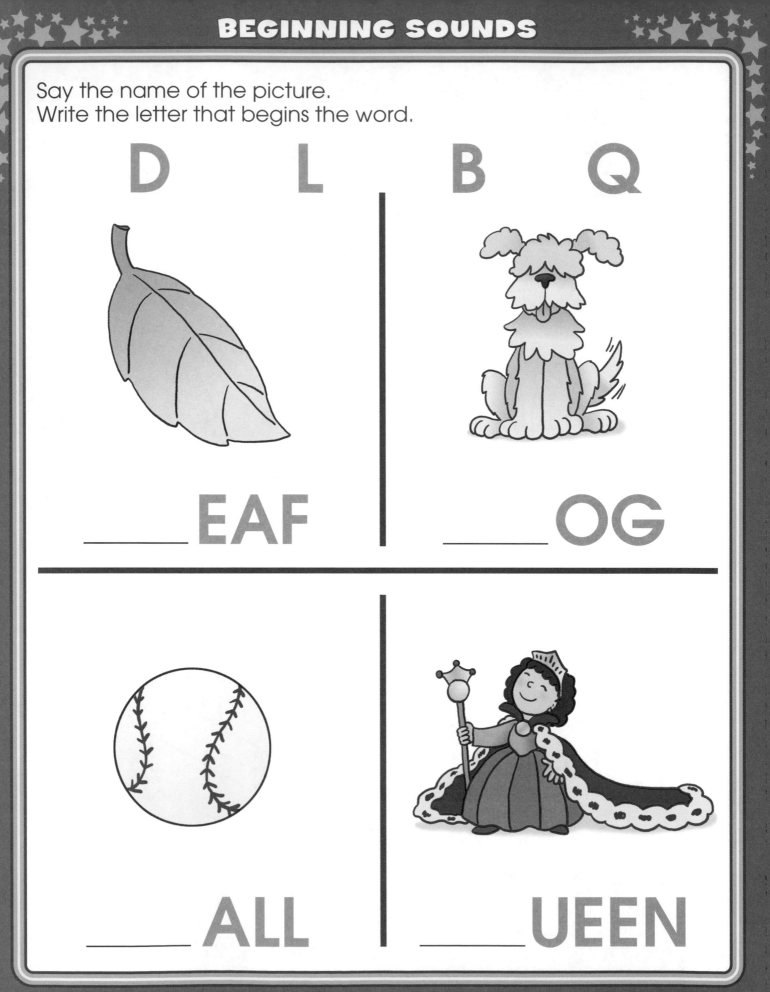

____EAF   ____OG

____ALL   ____UEEN

Say the name of the picture.
Write the letter that begins the word.

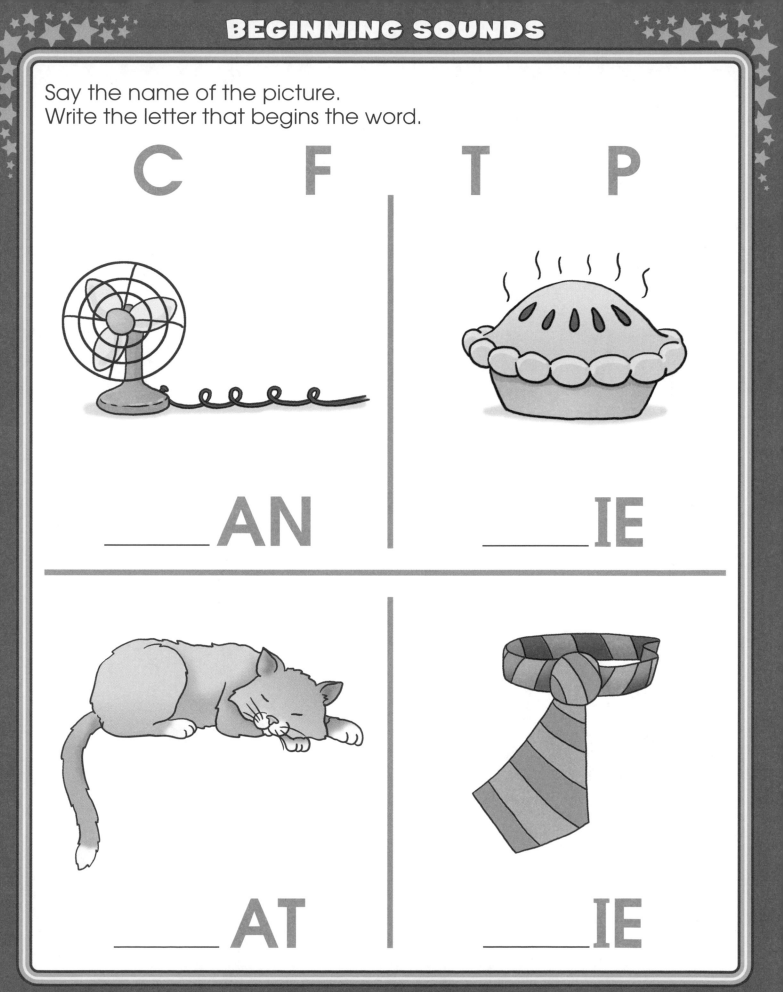

C F   T P

___AN   ___IE

___AT   ___IE

Say the name of the picture.
Write the letter that ends the word.

L R   D F

BE ____

SEA ____

CA ____

EL ____

Say the name of the picture.
Write the letter that ends the word.

S   T   O   K

ZER _____

BU _____

HA _____

BOO _____

Phonics

Say the name of the picture.
Write the letter that ends the word.

P   B   G   N

PI____   SU____

CU____   TU____

Say the name of the picture.
Write the letter that ends the word.

L   X   R   M

NAI____   FO____

BEA____   DRU____

Phonics

PRE-READING SKILLS

There is no ability more essential to your child's success in school than reading. Reading, and understanding what is read, is the key to all of the other subjects. This section will help your child develop important reading readiness skills. The section is divided into four parts:

- The Same or Different component will help your child learn to compare and contrast items. To do so, your child must look for significant details, which is a critical reading readiness skill.

- The Does It Belong? component will boost your child's confidence as he or she learns to classify and match objects. Recognizing likenesses and differences will prepare your child for reading and math.

- The Following Directions component will introduce positional words and review shapes, numbers, and colors. Learning to follow directions will build your child's confidence and prepare him or her for school.

- The Thinking Skills component will help your child practice a variety of critical reasoning skills. The exercises focus on organizing information, classifying, sequencing, and solving logic puzzles.

These are the **same**.

Circle **2** that are the **same**.

Pre-Reading Skills

SAME

Circle **2** that are the **same**.

Circle **2** that are the **same** in each group.

Circle **2** that are the **same**.

Circle **2** that are the **same** in each group.

Pre-Reading Skills

SAME

Circle the picture that is the **same** as the first one.

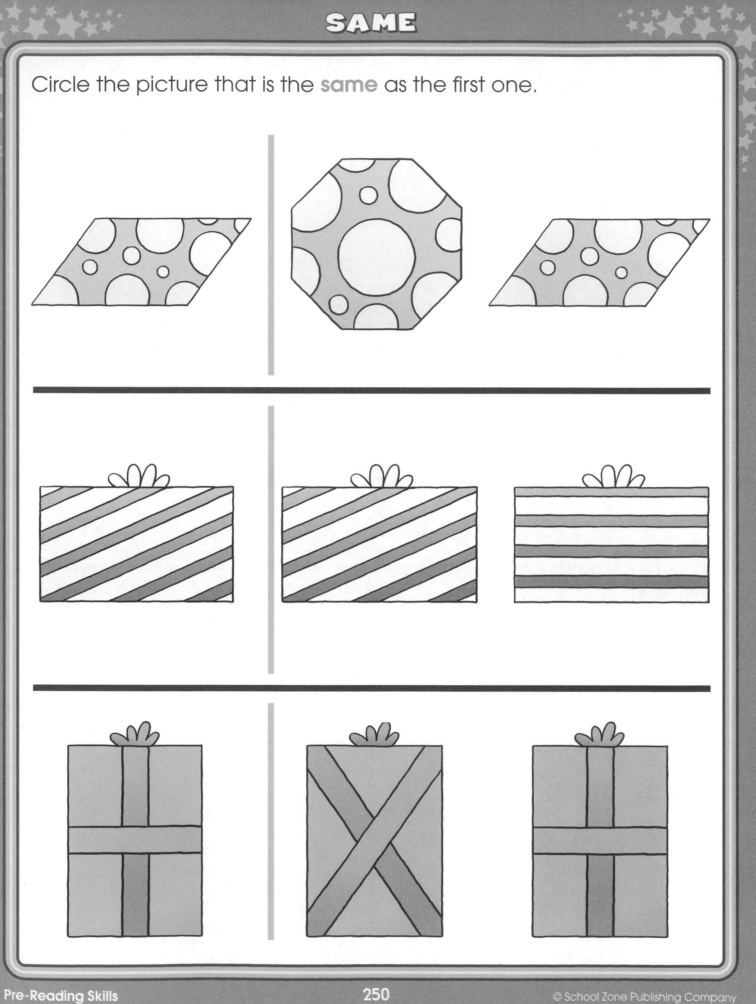

Circle the picture that is the **same** as the first one.

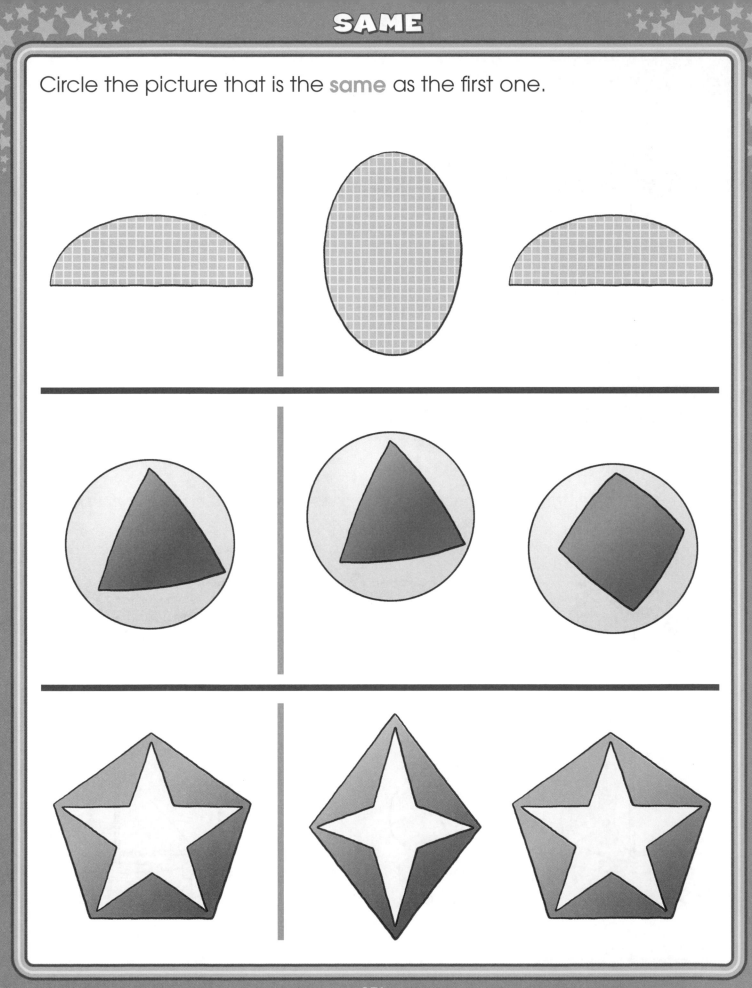

Pre-Reading Skills

One is different.

Circle the picture that is different.

Circle the picture that is **different**.

Circle the picture that is **different** in each group.

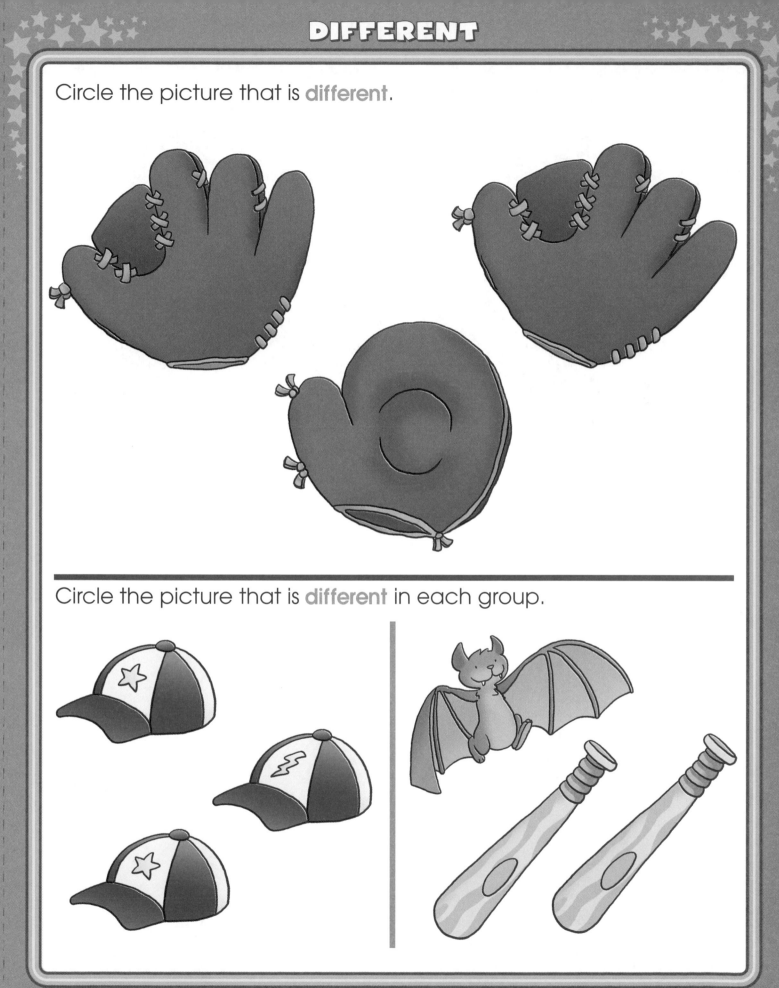

Pre-Reading Skills

Circle the picture that is **different**.

Circle the picture that is **different** in each group.

Circle the picture that is **different**.

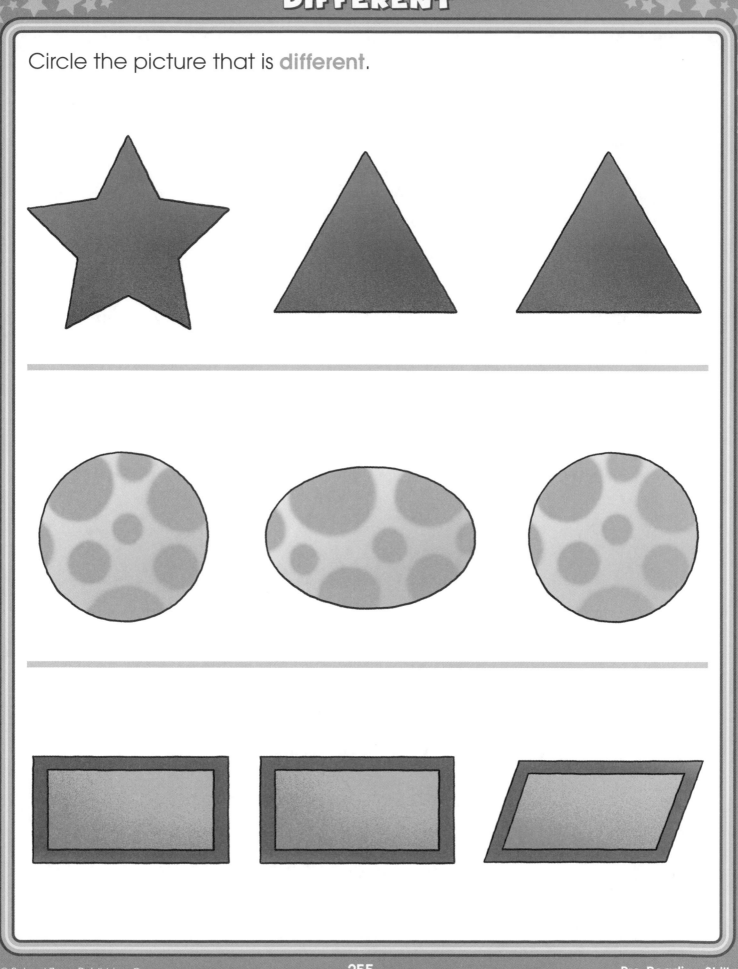

Pre-Reading Skills

Circle the picture that is **different**.

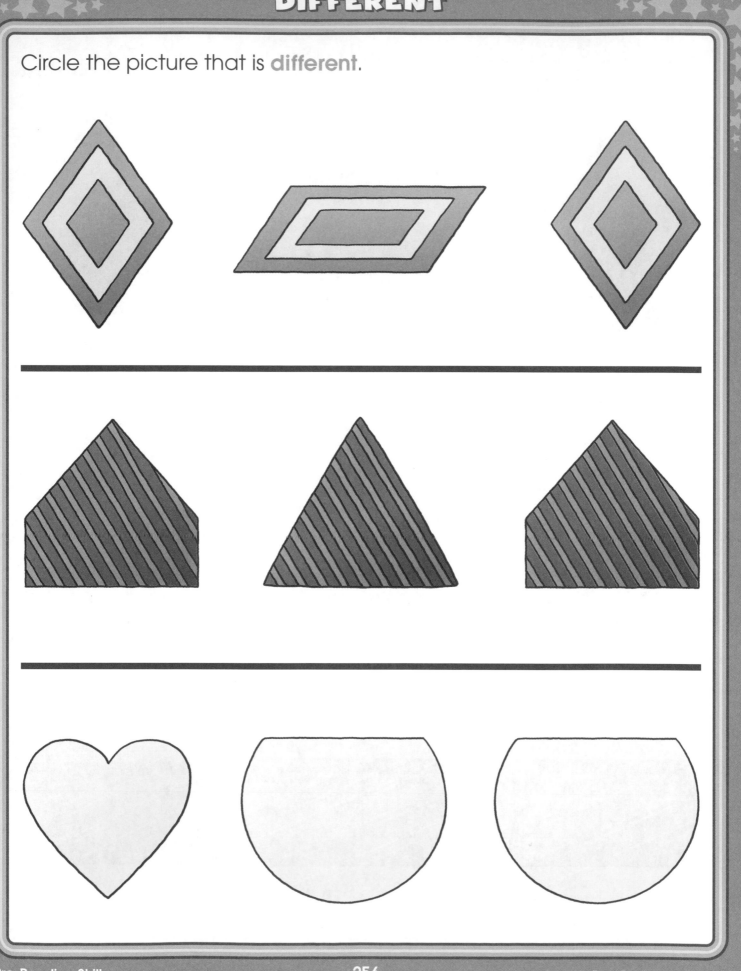

SAME SIZE

These are the **same size**.
Circle the picture that is the **same size** as the first one.

Pre-Reading Skills

SAME SIZE

Circle the picture that is the **same size** as the first one.

DIFFERENT SIZE

These  are the same size. This is a **different size**. Circle the picture that is a **different size**.

DIFFERENT SIZE

Circle the picture that is a **different size**.

This  is big. This is **bigger**.
Circle the picture that is **bigger** than the first one.

SMALLER

This  is small. This  is smaller.
Circle the picture that is smaller than the first one.

Circle the bird with the **long** pants.

Circle the bird with the **long** legs.

Pre-Reading Skills

Circle the dog with the **short** tail.

Circle the child with **short** hair.

belongs with .

Circle the picture that **belongs** with the first one.

Circle the picture that **belongs** with the first one.

Circle the picture that **belongs** with the first one.

Pre-Reading Skills

BELONGS

Circle the picture that **belongs** with the first one.

BELONGS

Circle **3** things that **belong** in the ice cream store.

Circle **3** things that **belong** in the school.

Circle **3** things that **belong** in the zoo.

Hippo

Lion

MONKEY

BELONGS

Circle **3** things that **belong** at the beach.

Circle the picture that **does not belong** in each group.

DOES NOT BELONG

Circle the picture that **does not** belong in each group.

DOES NOT BELONG

Circle the picture that **does not belong** in each group.

Circle the picture that **does not belong** in each group.

Circle what **does not belong** in the picture.

DOES NOT BELONG

Circle what **does not belong** in the picture.

Circle what **does not belong** in the picture.

Pre-Reading Skills

The  is **in** the 🏠.

Draw an ⬭ around who is **in** the 🛁.

Color the 🛁 orange.

Color the 🏐 green and purple.

The  is **out** of the ⌂.

Draw a ☐ around what is **out** of the ⬭.

Color the ⬭ green.

This  is going **up**.

X the that is going **up**.

Draw a —— from the to the .

This  is going **down**.

✔ the 🐬 that is going **down**.

Draw 4 🐟 .

The  is **on** the 's head.

✔ who is **on** the .

Draw a ——— from the to the .

The  is **off** the .

Draw a ☐ around the 🦋 that is **off** the 🌸 .

Draw 3 🦋 s.

The 🐭 is on **top**.

✔ the ▭ that is on **top**.

Draw 1 🎀 on the ▭ .

The ⚲ is on the **bottom**.

✔ who is on the **bottom**.

Draw 2 🌰s.

Color the 🐿s brown.

The  is **low** on the ⚖.

Draw a ☐ around who is **low** on the 🛝.

Color the ☀ yellow.

The  is **high** on the .

✔ who is **high** on the .

Draw a on the .

Pre-Reading Skills

The  is jumping **over** the 🐭 .

X the 🐔 that is going **over** the 🐱 .

Color the 🐱 red.

The 😮 is **under** the ☂.

✗ the 🐇 that is **under** the 🛒.

Draw 5 🥕s.

Pre-Reading Skills

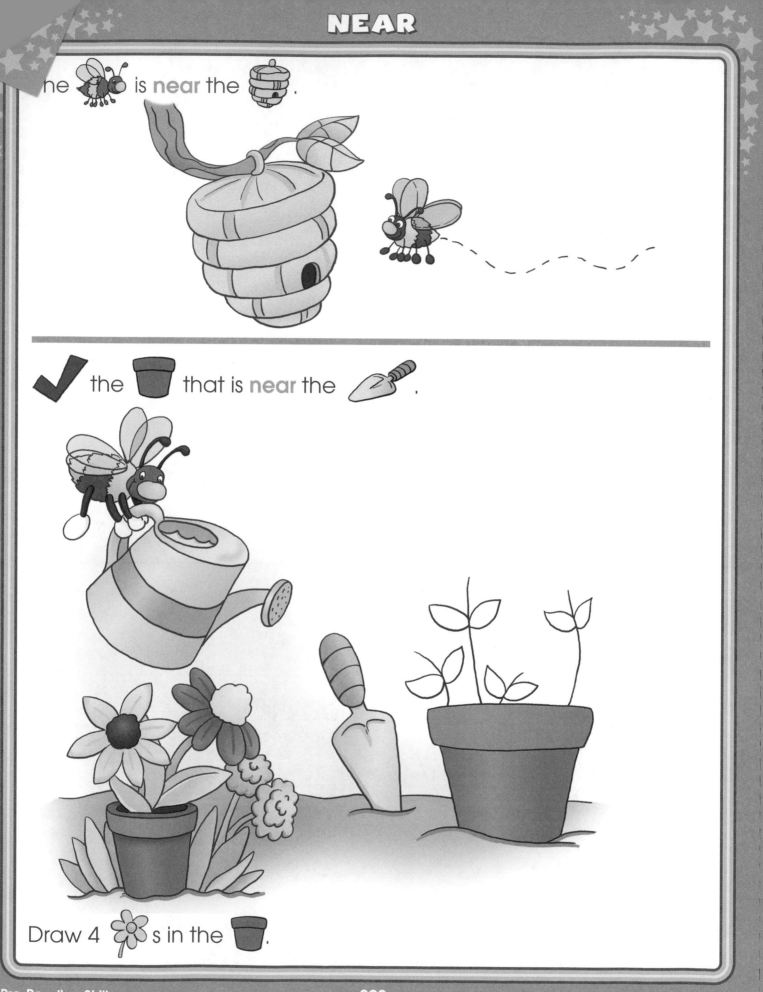

The is **near** the .

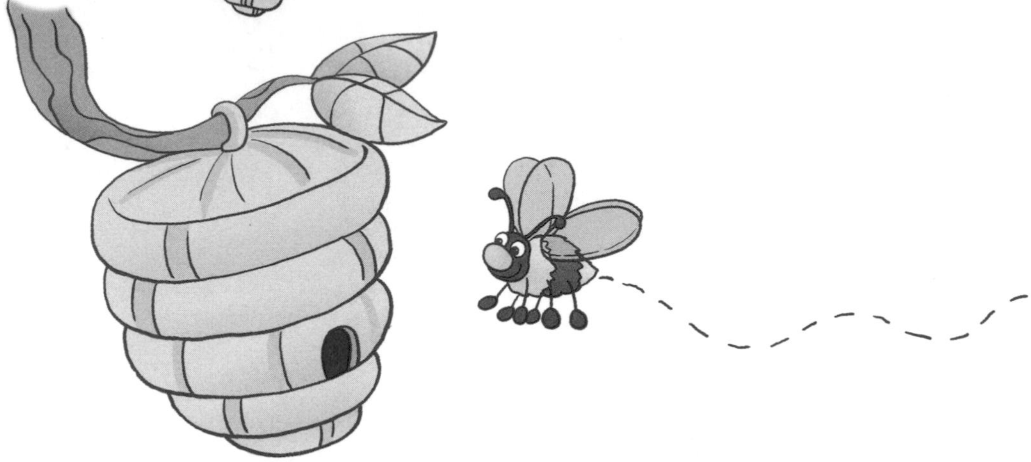

✓ the that is **near** the .

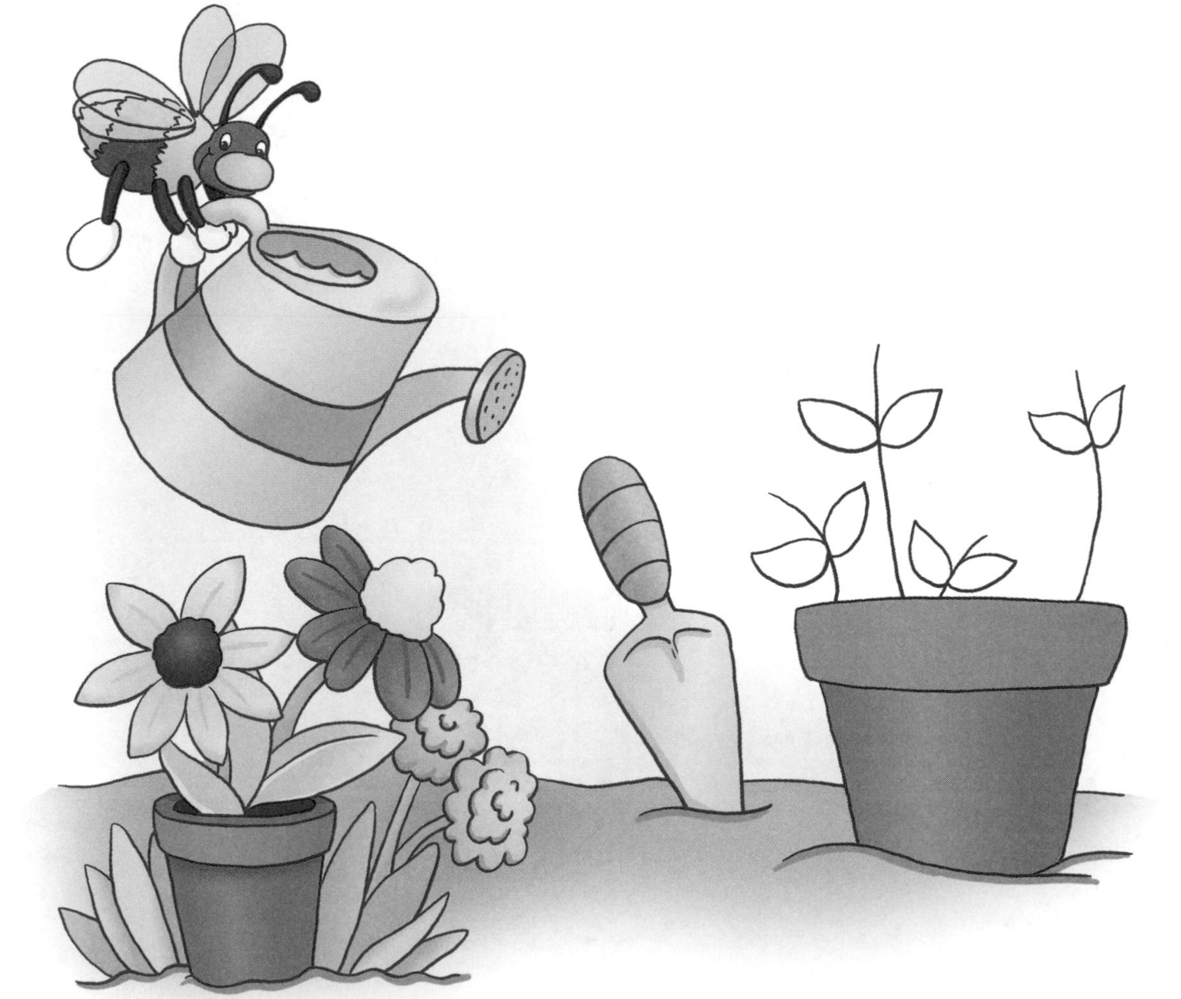

Draw 4 s in the .

FAR

The 🐰 is **far** from the 👹.

Draw a ⬭ around the 🌳 that is **far** from the 🐶.

Draw a ——— from the 🐦 to the 🪹.
Color the 🐶 black.

Pre-Reading Skills

The  is **in front of** the 🚚 .

Draw a ▭ around what is **in front of** the 🏢 .

Trace the △ on the 🏠 .

The  is **in back of** the .

Draw an ◯ around who is **in back of** the .

Draw 2 s.

Pre-Reading Skills

The  is **next to** the 🐦 .

✔ the 🐢 that is **next to** the 🦤 .

Color the 🎈 blue.

The  is **between** the 🐭🐭.

Draw a ▭ around who is **between**.

Color the 👕 purple.

Trace the ⌒.

Pre-Reading Skills

The  is turning **left**.

✓ the that is turning **left**.

Draw an apple on the plate.

The  is turning **right**.

Draw a ◺ around the 🐧 that is turning **right**.

Trace the ⌒ of the 🐧 turning **right**.

Circle what goes with **summer**.

Circle what goes with **winter**.

SENSE OF SMELL

Circle what you can **smell**.

Circle what you can **taste**.

Circle what you can **touch**.

Circle what you can **hear**.

EMOTIONS

Circle the picture that shows how you would **feel**.

PATTERNS

Draw the shape that comes **next**.

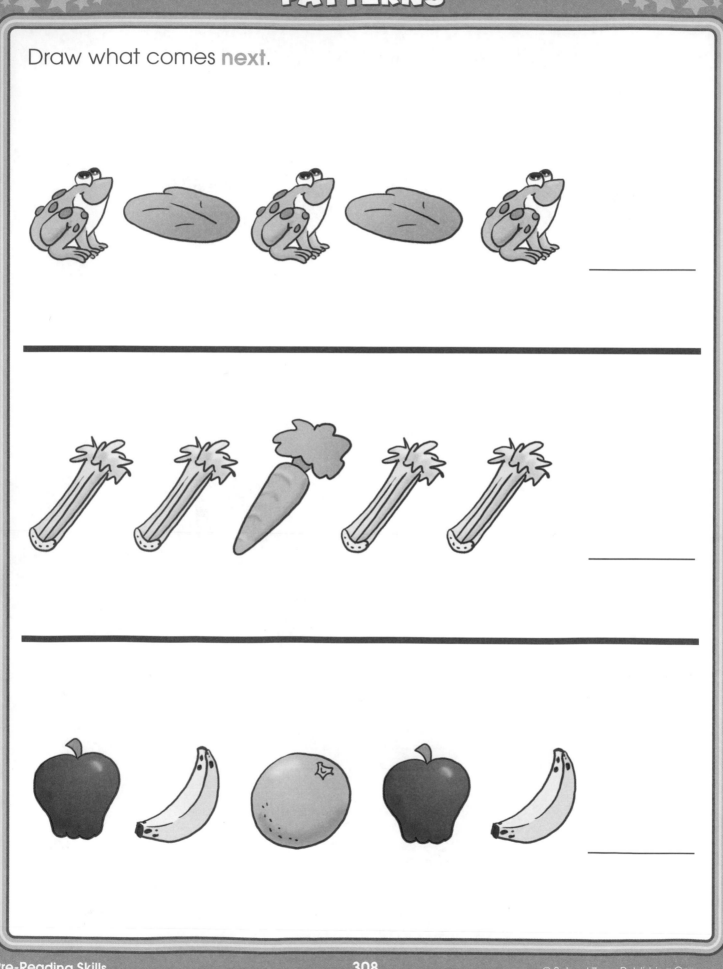

PATTERNS

Draw what comes **next**.

Circle the picture that shows why this happened.

Circle the picture that shows why this happened.

Write **1** by what happened **first**.
Write **2** by what happened **next**.
Write **3** by what happened **last**.

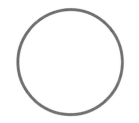
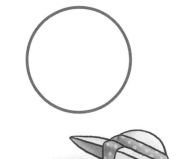
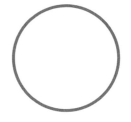

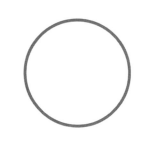

Pre-Reading Skills

STORY ORDER

Write **1** by what happened **first**.
Write **2** by what happened **next**.
Write **3** by what happened **last**.

STORY ORDER

Write **1** by what happened **first**.
Write **2** by what happened **next**.
Write **3** by what happened **last**.

Pre-Reading Skills

Circle the picture that completes the sentence.

is to _____ as _____ is to _____ .

is to _____ as _____ is to _____ .

Circle the picture that completes the sentence.

is to   as   is to _____.

WOOF!

is to   as   is to _____.

Which pet did Mia choose?
Circle the correct picture.

1. It cannot fly.

2. It is not gray.

3. It has a long tail.

Which house is Peter's?
Circle the correct picture.

1. It has a green door.

2. It is not pink.

3. It has two windows.

Read the clues.
Draw a line from each name to the correct clown.

1. Mac is between Ned and Jake.

2. Jake has a flower in his hat.

Ned   Jake   Mac

Read the clues.
Draw a line from each name to the correct dog.

1. Hero is on the bottom.

2. Rags is in the middle.

3. Paco is under Duke.

4. Where is Fido?

Rags

Duke

Paco

Hero

Fido

Preschool Barnyard

Art Studio

Let Rodney T. Rooster wake up your child's creativity with coloring book fun, or encourage your child to create his or her own masterpiece.

Dot-to-Dots

Your child will learn sequencing of the ABCs and 123s as he or she connects the dots and watches the pictures come to life.

Movies

Take a sneak peek at what's playing now. Your child will want to knock on this door again and again to watch these 12 captivating movies.

Educational Game

Behind this barn door, your child will discover an exciting game full of preschool fun. He or she will learn numbers, colors, shapes, and more down on the farm.

Jokes

Knock, knock. Who's there? This silly filly will tickle your child's funny bone with jokes and riddles. Don't forget to keep a lookout for a surprise delivery in today's mail!

Help

Does your child need some help? Does he or she need to know how to play a game? The question mark will lend a hand.

Meet Sherman Sheep and the rest of the barnyard buddies! They can't wait to show off the exciting activities tucked behind each door. Pencil-Pal Software combines educational content with sound, motion, and just the right amount of fun to help your child prepare for school success.

Educational Goal

This interactive software introduces important preschool skills through a variety of fun activities that appeal to different learning styles.

Educational Content

- Alphabet
- Numbers
- Letter and Number Sequencing
- Counting
- Classifying
- Shapes
- Colors

Developmental Skills

- Listening
- Following Directions
- Critical Thinking
- Problem Solving
- Eye-hand Coordination

Program Features

- The simple program design will allow your child to work independently.
- Creative themes, adorable characters, and playful melodies will appeal to your child.
- Audio and animated rewards will reinforce learning.
- Drawing, painting, and coloring activities will encourage creative learning.
- Jokes and movies will keep your child motivated.